The Light Within

What the Prophet Joseph Smith Taught Us about Personal Revelation

W. Jeffrey Marsh

Visit us at www.deseretbook.com

Library of Congress Cataloging-in-Publication Data

Marsh, W. Jeffrey.
The light within/W. Jeffrey Marsh.
p. cm.
Includes bibliographical references.
ISBN 1-57345-807-4
1. Holy Spirit. 2. Gifts, Spiritual—Church of Jesus Christ of Latter-day Saints. 3. Church of Jesus Christ of Latter-day Saints—Doctrines. 4. Smith, Joseph, 1805–1844. I. Title.
BX8643.H63 M27 2000
248.2'9—dc21 00-040442

Printed in the United States of America 42316-6695

10 9 8 7 6 5 4 3 2 1

For my father, mother, and grandmother

Contents

Preface

Throughout this book you will notice more verses of scripture, more quotations from sermons, and more personal experiences from the Prophet Joseph Smith regarding the principle of revelation and light from heaven than from any other individual. Joseph Smith was heaven-taught and angel-tutored and knew more about this subject than any other living person. In his marvelous generosity he shared as much as we were prepared to receive.

I am indebted to Deseret Book Company for their approval to pursue this study and especially to Cory Maxwell and Suzanne Brady for their help, encouragement, and editorial insights. Thanks also goes to Rebecca Chambers and Christine Graham for editorial assistance, Tom Hewitson for graphic design, and Tonya-Rae Facemyer for typesetting.

My deepest gratitude goes to my wife, Kathie, and our children for their constant love and support.

CHAPTER 1

Light from Heaven

Joseph Smith came to know the mind and will of God by studying holy writ and by having personal experiences with Deity. He learned to communicate with heaven by the language of the Spirit—personal revelation. Just before his martyrdom in 1844, he said, "I have the oldest book in my heart, even the gift of the Holy Ghost."[1]

The Prophet Joseph was tutored by angels, was instructed personally by the Savior, and was privileged to speak with God face to face. No other person in all of Christian history since the days of the apostles of Christ was as familiar with the spirit of revelation. In a day when religionists were claiming that the heavens were closed, Joseph Smith was bearing testimony that the veil had been opened again and that God was in fact speaking to prophets once more.

In 1839, Joseph Smith, Sidney Rigdon, and others visited Washington, D.C., to present the petitions for redress following the Saints' expulsion from Missouri. On their return trip to Nauvoo, they were invited to speak to some three thousand people in one of the largest churches in Philadelphia. President Rigdon addressed the congregation first. Fearful of their reaction, he carefully avoided any reference to visions and the coming of angels, upon which the Restoration rests.

According to Elder Parley P. Pratt, this hesitancy was so disconcerting to the Prophet Joseph that, when President Rigdon finished, "Brother Joseph arose like a lion about to roar; and being full of the Holy Ghost, spoke in great power, bearing testimony of the visions he had seen, the ministering of angels which he had enjoyed; and how he had found the plates of the Book of Mormon, and translated them by the gift and power of God. He commenced by saying: 'If nobody else had the courage to testify of so glorious a message from Heaven, and of the finding of so glorious a record, he felt to do it in justice to the people, and leave the event with God.'

"The entire congregation were astounded; electrified, as it were, and overwhelmed with the sense of the truth and power by which he spoke, and the wonders which he related. A lasting impression was made; many souls were gathered into the fold. And I bear witness, that he, by his faithful and powerful testimony, cleared his garments of their blood."[2]

When the Savior gave the keys of the kingdom to Peter, James, and John in the meridian of time, he declared that the rock upon which his Church was built was revelation from "my Father who is in heaven" (JST Matthew 16:18). In 1829, as resurrected beings, Peter, James, and John laid their hands on Joseph Smith's head and gave him those same keys. Thus, Joseph Smith, the latter-day seer was empowered from heaven to receive revelation. The Prophet "would unravel the scriptures," Wandle Mace observed, "and explain doctrine as no other man could. What had been mystery he made so plain it was no longer mystery."[3]

A Gift from God

Personal revelation—the light from heaven—is a gift from God. The ability to receive that light is also a gift placed deep within every human soul. It is an eternal part of our immortal natures. It is so much a part of us that we often take it for granted, but it is a unique and precious gift of light from God.

The light within is more than the light of Christ, or our conscience. It is the ability each of us has to receive communication from

God. The light within, as that term is used in this book, is personal revelation in all its forms, including the power of discernment that flows from the light of Christ; witnesses or testimony from the Holy Ghost; thoughts, feelings, impressions, or comforting assurances from the Holy Ghost; the gift and power of the Holy Ghost to sanctify our souls; the gifts, peace, and feelings of pure love accompanying the Spirit of the Lord; visits by angels; and visions, dreams, and revelations from God.

The light within is meat and drink for our souls. Every one of us may receive revelation from heaven and divine inspiration for our own benefit. In fact, this ability is so much a natural part of our being that many who receive such help and inspiration may be unaware of it (3 Nephi 9:20). Others who are more spiritually sensitive are aware of the source of this light, as was the prophet Alma, who declared, "I would not that ye should think that I know these things of myself, but it is the Spirit of God which is in me which maketh these things known unto me; for if I had not been born of God I should not have known these things" (Alma 38:6).

The light within, or revelation from heaven, provides the needed guidance to "lead the faithful to eternal salvation in the celestial kingdom."[4] Whether it is the light of Christ helping us understand gospel truths and find the gospel path that leads to eternal life, or the greater gift of the Holy Ghost directing us in life's most critical decisions, the light within (inspiration from heaven) will guide us safely through life's treacherous shoals. It touches our hearts and enlightens our minds. It teaches us the difference between right and wrong. If followed, it will rise like the sun in the morning until it becomes a light shining in the strength of the noonday sun.

The process begins by our following the light of Christ, which leads us to receive the Holy Ghost, who will reveal the Son, who will then reveal the Father. Those who receive that Spirit and live in obedience to it will have all things past and present brought to their remembrance, and be shown things to come. In that manner, the light within can lead us to all truth and reacquaint us with our Eternal Father and His divine Son, the Redeemer, from whom all light radiates. It will prepare us for the glorious return of Christ to the earth. And, most importantly, it will lead us to the ordinances and covenants we need to make and keep in order to lay hold on eternal life and reenter God's presence. The Lord is no respecter of persons. Obedience to the light revealed from heaven and received through personal righteousness leads to the salvation the Savior offers us.

The doctrine of Christ, which he testified he received from the Father, is to prepare us to receive more light through faith, repentance, baptism, receiving the gift of the Holy Ghost, and righteous living (3 Nephi 11:32–35). Of those who obey this doctrine, the Savior said, "They are they who shall inherit the kingdom of God" (3 Nephi 11:33). The Prophet Joseph Smith understood that without revelation from God, all mankind would continue to remain unenlightened: "It is not to be wondered at that men should be ignorant, in a great measure, of the principles of salvation, and more especially of the nature, office, power, influence, gifts, and blessings of the gift of the Holy Ghost; when we consider that the human family have been enveloped in gross darkness and ignorance for many centuries past, without revelation."[5]

Heavenly Help

None of us can reach the celestial kingdom without the mercy, merits, and grace of our Lord Jesus Christ and his atonement. Neither can we get there without the help of the Holy Ghost. At the Last Supper, the Savior taught the Twelve Apostles how the Holy Ghost would know how to help each of us. "When he, the Spirit of truth, is come, he will guide you into all truth: *for he shall not speak of himself*; but whatsoever he shall hear, that shall he speak: and he will shew you things to come. He shall glorify me: for he shall receive of mine, and shall shew it unto you" (John 16:13–14; emphasis added).

Because of his atoning sacrifice, the Savior knows all of our weaknesses, temptations, trials, infirmities, shortcomings, and sins (Alma 7:11–13). He knows precisely what help and revelation we need, and he imparts it to the Holy Ghost, who then reveals it to us (John 16:13–14). Through the power of Christ's infinite atonement and with the help of the Holy Ghost, all of us have the opportunity for eternal life. That is our Heavenly Father's plan—the "great plan of the Eternal

God" (Alma 34:9), the "great plan of happiness" (Alma 42:8), which the Father has provided for us.

The Prophet Joseph Smith learned that "a knowledge of the things of God . . . can only be known by the Spirit of God."[6] The work before us, then, is to prepare ourselves to receive this great gift and to obey God with all purpose of heart, said Elder Orson Pratt, "that we may be visited with more and more of that divine spirit, the Comforter, the Holy Ghost which we had confirmed upon us, by authority, through the laying on of hands. That Comforter should be nourished and cherished in our hearts. We should not grieve it. We should listen to its whisperings, and we should seek after more light, and knowledge, and truth."[7] Elder Boyd K. Packer taught that very little else compares with this most lasting reward, that of having the Spirit: "The choicest pearl, the one of great price, is to learn at an early age how one is guided by the Spirit of the Lord, a supernal gift. Indeed it is a guide and a protection."[8]

If we can and often do receive revelation, why do some feel as if they never have? The problem is one of connections, of learning to recognize the spirit of revelation. We can learn to recognize the promptings of the Spirit in our own lives by studying the teachings and experiences of the Prophet Joseph Smith, who taught more than any other person about the gifts and blessings of the Spirit.

Joseph Smith and Light from Heaven

In every gospel dispensation, there has been at least one individual to whom God the Eternal Father has revealed himself and to whom he has introduced his Only Begotten Son, Jesus Christ. God's Spirit abides with them (Moses 6:26). They are invited to walk with God and to put their lives in harmony with his Spirit (Moses 6:34). They are commanded to bear witness of the Father and of the Son by the power of the Holy Ghost so that faith might increase on the earth (D&C 1:17–18, 21). By virtue of their testimony, others are inspired to seek after God and come to know for themselves that the witness these choice and chosen servants bear is true. Men and women are thereby empowered to lay hold on eternal life and exercise faith in God. This gives them the hope (the expectation) of a place in a better world (the celestial kingdom), and anchors their souls throughout their mortal lives to God and works of righteousness (Ether 12:4).

In this dispensation, the dispensation of the fulness of times, the first witness who saw and came to know the Father and the Son was Joseph Smith. Much has been written, and rightly so, about Joseph's seeing God the Eternal Father and His Son Jesus Christ in the Sacred Grove (Joseph Smith–History 1:15–20). The First Vision was the greatest revelation given since the Savior's mortal ministry. Beginning with that revelation, the Prophet Joseph was taught about and received understanding through the Spirit. Indeed, the Spirit of the Lord was greatly manifest throughout Joseph's life. One convert, James Palmer, said of the Prophet, "He looked and had the appearance of one that was heaven born while preaching or as though as he had been sent from the heavenly worlds on a divine mission."[9]

Many others shared similar testimonies: "Truly when he spoke light, wisdom and intelligence flowed from his mouth in a way not to be heard from an uninspired man," John Spiers testified. "Sabbath after Sabbath I heard Set forth the order of the Kingdom of God in a way well calculated to gladden the hearts of those who were seeking truth for their guide."[10] Brigham Young said that before he met Joseph Smith, "all the priests of the day could not tell me anything correct about heaven, hell, God, angels, or devils: they were as blind as Egyptian darkness. When I saw Joseph Smith, he took heaven, figuratively speaking, and brought it down to earth; and he took the earth, brought it up, and opened up, in plainness and simplicity, the things of God; and that is the beauty of his mission."[11] Wandle Mace wrote, "I ask, who understood anything about these things until Joseph being inspired from on high touched the key and unlocked the door of these mysteries of the kingdom."[12]

Where did Joseph Smith receive the power and ability to speak with such confidence about heavenly things? The source of the Prophet's authority and revelation was God. Joseph was also visited by various angelic beings who gave him knowledge, keys, and powers long withheld from men (D&C 128:21). President John Taylor testified that Joseph Smith "learned by communication from the heavens."[13] Joseph bore witness that he had "received many visits from the angels of God unfolding the majesty and glory of the events that should transpire in the last days."[14]

Beginning with his simple declaration at age fourteen that "when the light rested upon me, I saw . . ." (Joseph Smith–History 1:17) the Prophet Joseph Smith immediately stood preeminent. During his lifetime, he received more light and intelligence from heaven than any other mortal since the death of the early apostles. Whether we wish to learn about the gifts of the Spirit, the quiet promptings of the still small voice, the visitation of angels, dreams, open visions of God in heaven, or revelation of new scripture, Joseph Smith is uniquely qualified to teach us. The Lord promised him that "the ends of the earth shall inquire after thy name . . . while the pure in heart, and the wise, and the noble, and the virtuous, shall seek counsel, and authority, and blessings constantly from under thy hand" (D&C 122:1–2).

The Prophet Joseph Smith grew to understand the gift and power of the Holy Ghost and experienced those blessings on many occasions. The life, teachings, and revelations of the Prophet Joseph Smith can teach us about the mission, messages, and miracles of the Spirit of God and how to make them a greater part of our daily lives. Brigham Young commented on the debt of gratitude we owe to the Prophet Joseph: "What I have received from the Lord, I have received by Joseph Smith; he was the instrument made use of. If I drop him, I must drop these principles; they have not been revealed, declared, or explained by any other man since the days of the Apostles."[15]

The keys Joseph Smith held were permanently established on the earth and are held by the living prophet today. As a result, prophets, seers, revelators, general authorities, and Church leaders all share, in their respective offices, the spiritual mantle restored through the Prophet Joseph Smith.

A most inspiring message of the Restoration is that the light of revelation can also rest on us, so that we too can see "things as they really are, and . . . things as they really will be" (Jacob 4:13). The light from heaven cascades down to every member who enters into the kingdom of God by baptism, receives by the laying on of hands the gift of the Holy Ghost, and lives in obedience to the promptings of that Spirit.

The Promise of Light from Heaven

Through the Prophet Joseph Smith was revealed more information about the Spirit of God than through any other person. He understood perfectly what it meant to be led by the Spirit. He knew precisely what we have to do to receive the gifts bestowed by the Holy Ghost. The quantity of all he received is impressive but even more so is the quality. Joseph promised that every person is privileged to experience the light from heaven. Our Heavenly Father deals with all his children fairly. He delights to pour out light and truth upon all those who will receive it.

To all who will hear, the Prophet Joseph gave this glorious promise: "Fellow sojourners upon earth, it is your privilege to purify yourselves and come up to the same glory, and see for yourselves, and know for yourselves. Ask, and it shall be given you; seek and ye shall find; knock, and it shall be opened unto you."[16]

Notes

1. Smith, *Teachings*, 349.
2. *Autobiography of Parley Parker Pratt*, 298–99.
3. Mace, Autobiography, 101–2; as cited in Black, Telford, and Averett, *Nauvoo*, 62.
4. *Guide to the Scriptures*, 209.
5. Smith, *Teachings*, 242.
6. Smith, *Teachings*, 242; see also Jacob 4:8; 1 Corinthians 2.
7. Pratt, *Journal of Discourses*, 21:206.
8. Packer, *That All May Be Edified*, 342.
9. James Palmer, *Reminiscences*, as cited in *Church History in the Fulness of Times*, 259.
10. John Spiers, Autobiography and Diary, unpaged; as cited in Jessee, "Priceless Words and Fallible Memories," 20.
11. Young, *Journal of Discourses*, 5:332.
12. Mace, Autobiography, 101–2; as cited in Black, Telford, and Averett, *Nauvoo*, 62.
13. Taylor, *Journal of Discourses*, 20:174–75.

14. Smith, *History of the Church*, 4:537.
15. Young, *Journal of Discourses*, 6:279.
16. Smith, *Teachings*, 12–13.

CHAPTER 2

Understanding the Light Within

The light within our soul emanates from God. It enlightens our eyes and quickens our understandings (D&C 88:11). It is a channel through which the Holy Ghost can communicate spiritual and secular knowledge to the world. It inspires the minds of men and women to create new things and bring forth new inventions. It imparts knowledge and a degree of intelligence to the spirits of all the children of men, precisely as Job described: "There is a spirit in man: and the inspiration of the Almighty giveth them understanding" (Job 32:8).

Similar words are used in the scriptures to describe this light—the Spirit of God, the Holy Ghost, the gift of the Holy Ghost, and the light of Christ. It can be confusing when such terms as "the Spirit," "the Spirit of the Lord," "the Spirit of Truth," and the "light of truth" are used synonymously. Although they all work together to bless us, there are differences among the light of Christ, the Holy Ghost, the gift of the Holy Ghost, and the gifts of the Spirit. Through the revelations given to the Prophet Joseph Smith and other latter-day prophets, we can better distinguish between these separate and distinct entities and understand more precisely how to obtain blessings from them.

The Light of Christ

The term "light of Christ" can only be found in the scriptures of the Restoration (Alma 28:14; Moroni 7:18; D&C 88:7), even though the principles on which it operates are often described in the Bible. Those who cultivate the light of Christ by noticing its operations in their lives and following its promptings are those who hear the voice of the Shepherd. "My sheep hear my voice" (John 10:27). One way all of us can hear God's voice is to follow the light of Christ, that "sixth sense" in our souls, our conscience.

The light of Christ is not a person. It is, rather, the divine energy or influence emanating from God which proceeds through Jesus Christ to the world (D&C 50:27). It is the inspiration of the Almighty that he pours out upon his children (Joel 2:28–29). The light of Christ is given to all who enter mortality. Elder Bruce R. McConkie said the light of Christ "defies description and is beyond mortal comprehension. It is in us and in all things; it is around us and around all things; it fills the earth and the heavens and the universe. It is everywhere, in all immensity, without exception; it is an indwelling, immanent, ever-present, never-absent spirit. It has neither shape nor form nor personality. It is not an entity nor a person nor a personage. It has no agency, does not act independently, and exists not to act but to be acted upon."[1]

The Lord taught the Prophet Joseph Smith that the light of Christ proceeds "from the presence of God to fill the immensity of space—the light which is in all things, which giveth life to all things" (D&C 88:12–13). It fills the universe but it also fills our souls. It is the "life and the light of the world" (Alma 38:9), and it can be the light of our lives. The Savior declared that he is the source of this light: "I am the light of the world: he that followeth me shall not walk in darkness, but shall have the light of life" (John 8:12). The scriptures testify of this truth: "The Lord is my light and my salvation" (Psalm 27:1). "O send out thy light and thy truth: let them lead me" (Psalm 43:3). "God is the Lord, which hath shewed us light" (Psalm 118:27). "For thou wilt light my candle: the Lord my God will enlighten my darkness" (Psalm 18:28).

The light of Christ functions on many different levels. In plants it manifests itself as sunlight and photosynthesis, in animals as instinct, in our eyes as the light by which we see, and in our hearts as moral reason and conscience. To the righteous it becomes the means of revelation from the Holy Ghost. Many people mistake the light of Christ for God himself and as such, regardless of the name they have chosen for God, worship the light of Christ as if it were God. Mortals seem prone to worship God's creations rather than the Creator himself. Too many worship displays of God's power rather than worshipping him as the source of that power.

The light of Christ is a great influence for good in the lives of all people. It helps men, women, and children discern between good and evil. As we are obedient to the light within, our spirits become more sensitive to promptings of the still small voice of the Spirit. The light of Christ prepares a person to receive the Holy Ghost. It helps people understand gospel truths when they hear them (D&C 93:28–29, 31–32, 40, 42). It is the means by which individuals recognize and learn spiritual things. It invites everyone not only to do good but also to partake of God's goodness: "Wherefore," Moroni pleaded, "I beseech of you . . . that ye should search diligently in the light of Christ that ye may know good from evil; and if ye will lay hold upon every good thing, and condemn it not, ye certainly will be a child of Christ" (Moroni 7:19).

If its influence is not suppressed, the light of Christ will lead individuals to the fulness of the gospel of Jesus Christ, through which they can receive the greater gift of the Holy Ghost: "And the Spirit giveth light to every man that cometh into the world; and the Spirit enlighteneth every man through the world, that hearkeneth to the voice of the Spirit. And every one that hearkeneth to the voice of the Spirit cometh unto God, even the Father. And the Father teacheth him of the covenant" (D&C 84:46–48). President Joseph Fielding Smith explained, "If a man who has never heard the gospel will hearken to the teachings and manifestations of the Spirit of Christ, or the Light of Truth, which come to him, often spoken of as conscience . . . it will lead him eventually to the fulness of the gospel."[2]

The Prophet Joseph Smith was taught: "My voice is Spirit; my

Spirit is truth; truth abideth and hath no end; and if it be in you it shall abound. And if your eye be single to my glory, your whole bodies shall be filled with light, and there shall be no darkness in you; and that body which is filled with light comprehendeth all things. Therefore, sanctify yourselves that your minds become single to God" (D&C 88:66–68). "He that keepeth [the Lord's] commandments receiveth truth and light, until he is glorified in truth and knoweth all things" (D&C 93:28).

We can learn to be more receptive to the Spirit. Prophets have pleaded with God's children to learn to walk always in this light: "O house of Jacob," Isaiah cried, "come ye, and let us walk in the light of the Lord" (Isaiah 2:5). It is the quest of a lifetime to learn how to do this. A favorite Primary hymn contains this expression of gratitude about being guided by the light of the Lord:

Teach me to walk in the light of his love;
Teach me to pray to my Father above;
Teach me to know of the things that are right;
Teach me, teach me to walk in the light.

Father in Heaven, we thank thee this day
For loving guidance to show us the way.
Grateful, we praise thee with songs of delight!
Gladly, gladly we'll walk in the light.[3]

The Holy Ghost

The Holy Ghost is different from the light of Christ. The Holy Ghost is a real being in the form of a person. Joseph Smith taught that the Holy Ghost is a personage of spirit (D&C 130:22) who does not yet have a body or tabernacle of flesh and bones but who one day will.[4] "He does not and cannot transform himself into any other form or image than that of the Man whom he is."[5] That is why the Prophet Joseph taught that the Holy Ghost did not appear as a dove at the baptism of Jesus but that the dove was a sign that the Holy Ghost was present.[6] The Holy Ghost is the third member of the Godhead, separate and distinct from the Father and the Son (D&C 130:22).

Because he is a person, the Holy Ghost can only be in one place at one time. But his influence can be felt, like the rays of the sun, everywhere at once. His power and influence are manifest over all the earth simultaneously.[7] The Holy Ghost ministers to those in the human family who love the truth. He speaks to each person on the earth who is worthy to receive his promptings, and each one receives the message uniquely meant for him.[8]

The Holy Ghost performs vital roles in God's plan for our salvation: bearing record of the Father and the Son, revealing the truth of all things, and sanctifying those who have repented and been baptized. He may be "regarded as the minister of the Godhead, carrying into effect the decision of the Supreme Council [the Godhead]."[9] He partakes of the things of the Father and the Son and teaches them to those who keep their covenants made in the waters of baptism. What we learn from the Holy Ghost is precisely what the Father would have us know. President Brigham Young noted that the Holy Ghost never acts independently of God: "Not a desire, act, wish, or thought does the Holy Ghost indulge in contrary to that which is dictated by the Father."[10]

The Holy Ghost is received only when a person has repented and been baptized into the kingdom of God.[11] The Holy Ghost "stands as a guardian . . . to see that the light of the Spirit cannot be accessed by those who are not fully obedient to the principles of the law."[12]

The Holy Ghost is a witness, or testator.[13] He bears witness of the Father, of the Son, and of all truth: "And by the power of the Holy Ghost ye may know the truth of all things" (Moroni 10:5). Thus, he guides true disciples by showing them things to come, revealing the past and making known the hidden treasures of the kingdom of God.[14]

"No man can receive the Holy Ghost without receiving revelations," the Prophet Joseph Smith taught. "The Holy Ghost is a revelator."[15] To receive the Holy Ghost is to receive inspiration and revelation. "The Spirit of God speaking to the spirit of man has power to impart truth with greater effect and understanding than the truth can be imparted by personal contact even with heavenly beings."[16] That light led the Prophet Joseph Smith to seek after the spirit of revelation and to inquire of the Lord. As Joseph Smith pondered James 1:5, the light of Christ enlightened his mind and the Holy Ghost enlarged his soul: "Never," he said, "did any passage of scripture come with more power to the heart of man than this did at this time to mine. It seemed to enter with great force into every feeling of my heart. I reflected on it again and again, knowing that if any person needed wisdom from God, I did; for how to act I did not know, and unless I could get more wisdom than I then had, I would never know" (Joseph Smith–History 1:12). The experience was a "revelation directing him to receive a revelation."[17]

The revelations from the Holy Ghost draw us closer to God. To know God is to obtain the key, or secret, of eternal life: "And this is life eternal, that they might know thee the only true God, and Jesus Christ, whom thou hast sent" (John 17:3). There is no other way or means to obtain this knowledge except by revelation from the Holy Ghost: "Behold, great and marvelous are the works of the Lord. How unsearchable are the depths of the mysteries of him; and it is impossible that man should find out all his ways. And no man knoweth of his ways save it be revealed unto him; wherefore . . . despise not the revelations of God" (Jacob 4:8). "Salvation," Joseph Smith said, "cannot come without revelation."[18]

The Holy Ghost knows all things (D&C 35:19). We can receive help and individual revelation regarding all aspects of our lives, including callings, children, college, careers, and difficult choices. He can make all things manifest to us for our well-being (Moses 8:24). The Holy Ghost speaks "of things as they really are, and of things as they really will be" (Jacob 4:13). He also knows things as they really were and has the ability to bring all things to our remembrance, including things we learned and knew before we were born (John 14:26). Brigham Young said, "When true doctrines are advanced, though they may be new to the hearers, yet the principles contained in them are perfectly natural and easy to be understood, so much so that the hearers often imagine that they had always known them. This arises from the influence of the Spirit of Truth upon the spirit of intelligence that is within each person. The influence that comes from heaven is all the time teaching the children of men."[19]

President Joseph F. Smith referred to this process as a spiritual awakening: "All those salient truths which come home so forcibly to the head and heart seem but the awakening of the memories of the spirit. Can we know anything here that we did not know before we came? Are not the means of knowledge in the first estate equal to those of this? . . .

"But in coming here, we forgot all, that our agency might be free indeed, to choose good or evil, that we might merit the reward of our own choice and conduct. But by the power of the Spirit, in the redemption of Christ, through obedience, we often catch a spark from the awakened memories of the immortal soul, which lights up our whole being as with the glory of our former home."[20]

The Holy Ghost is an enlightener, a comforter, a justifier, and a sanctifier. He sanctifies and cleanses, through the power of the atonement of Jesus Christ, those who repent of their sins and are baptized by a legal administrator: "Now this is the commandment: Repent, all ye ends of the earth, and come unto me and be baptized in my name, that ye may be sanctified by the reception of the Holy Ghost, that ye may stand spotless before me at the last day" (3 Nephi 27:20).

Having been taught by Joseph Smith about the Holy Ghost's power to purify souls, Elder Orson Pratt wrote: "Water Baptism is only a preparatory cleansing of the believing penitent; it is only a condition of a cleansing from sin; whereas, the Baptism of fire and the Holy Ghost cleanses more thoroughly, by renewing the inner man, and by purifying the affections, desires, and thoughts which have long been habituated in the impure ways of sin. Without the aid of the Holy Ghost, a person who has long been accustomed to love sin, and whose affections and desires have long run with delight in the degraded channel of vice, would have but very little power to change his mind, at once, from its habituated course, and to walk in newness of life. Though his sins may have been cleansed away, yet so great is the force of habit, that he would, without being renewed by the Holy Ghost, be easily overcome, and contaminated again by sin. Hence, it is infinitely important that the affections and desires should be, in a measure, changed and renewed, so as to cause him to hate that which he before loved, and to love that which he before hated: to thus renew the mind of man is the work of the Holy Ghost."[21]

The King James Version of the Bible renders 1 John 3:9 as "Whosoever is born of God doth not commit sin . . . and he cannot sin, because he is born of God." The Joseph Smith Translation renders this verse as "Whosoever is born of God *doth not continue in sin;* for the Spirit of God remaineth in him; and *he cannot continue in sin,* because he is born of God, having received that holy Spirit of promise" (JST 1 John 3:9; emphasis added).

The companionship of the Holy Ghost purifies and cleanses our souls, but it also helps us turn, permanently, away from sin. Elder Bruce R. McConkie stated: "All men sin, before and after baptism, but those saints who strive to keep the commandments, and are continually repenting and returning to the Lord, no longer continue in that course of sinful rebellion against God and his laws which was their lot before they were baptized for the remission of sins. Church members who do so continue in sin are members in name only; they do not receive the companionship of the Holy Ghost, through whose revelations alone can the Lord be 'known.'"[22] Elder McConkie also said: "So simple a passage as John 17:3 ['This is life eternal, that they might know thee the only true God, and Jesus Christ, whom thou hast sent'] has a limited meaning for all men, but it is a celestial beacon of blazing light to us. From it we learn that to know God and Christ is to be like them—thinking what they think, speaking what they speak, doing what they do—all of which knowledge is beyond the capacity of an unenlightened mind to receive" ("The Bible—a Sealed Book," 37).

Receiving the Holy Ghost

The ultimate goal of all teaching in the Church and in our homes is to prepare hearts to receive the Spirit. That is why the Savior is the greatest of all teachers. He taught "as one having authority" (Matthew 7:29), not only because he was the Son of God but because he taught the truth with power and in a way that the Holy Ghost could bear witness of what he said. Five minutes of being instructed by the Spirit of the Lord will have a greater and more powerful effect than an entire lifetime of study.[23]

In a revelation to the Prophet Joseph Smith, the Savior commanded parents to "bring up [their] children in light and truth" (D&C 93:40). Elder Henry B. Eyring described how we might prepare the way so that our families can experience powerful teaching moments with the Spirit: "Even before baptism, a child or an adult can have the Holy Ghost testify to their hearts of sacred truth. They must act on that testimony to retain it, but it will guide them toward goodness, and it can lead them to accept and keep the covenants which will in time bring them the companionship of the Holy Ghost. . . . Since it is the Holy Ghost who testifies of sacred truth, we can do at least three things to make that experience more likely for our families. First, we can teach some sacred truth. Then we can testify that we know what we have taught is true. And then we must act so that those who hear our testimony see that our actions conform with what we said was true. The Holy Ghost will then confirm to them the truth of what we said and that we knew it to be true. That is how a legacy of testimony is created, preserved, and transmitted in a family. It isn't easy, but ordinary people have done it."[24]

Elder Gene R. Cook observed that "the greatest need the Church has is for inspired mothers and fathers who teach with the power of the Holy Ghost to touch the hearts of their children, to change their hearts and cause them to repent and draw closer to the Lord."[25] The mission of the Holy Ghost is to help us draw closer to the Lord by doing the following:

Bear record of the Father and the Son (D&C 20:27).

Teach us the peace-giving things of the kingdom, including peace of mind and a clear conscience (John 14:26).

Give us comfort (John 14:26–27).

Show us things to come (John 16:13).

Bring all things to our remembrance (John 14:26).

Like a compass, guide us to truth and bear strong testimony of the gospel (Moroni 10:5).

Reveal the deceptions of Satan (D&C 45:57).

Lead us to Christ and, eventually, back into the presence of God.[26]

Glorify the Savior (John 16:14).

Direct leaders in conducting Church meetings (D&C 42:16).

Reprove sins (John 16:8).

Touch our hearts (D&C 50:13–22).

Give us the very words we need to speak in the very moment we need them (D&C 100:5–8).

Enlighten our minds, or clarify our understanding (Alma 32:28; D&C 6:15).

Enable angels to speak to us (2 Nephi 32:3).

Convey spiritual gifts (D&C 46).

Confirm our wise decisions (2 Nephi 32:5; D&C 9:7–9).

Discern and reveal the thoughts of others (Alma 10:17; 18:18, 35).

Sanctify us and make us clean and pure (Alma 13:12).

Prompt us when we pray (D&C 46:30).

Show us all things that we should do (2 Nephi 32:2–5).

Cause people to prophesy (D&C 42:16).

Cause Church leaders to speak the will, mind, word, and the voice of the Lord (D&C 68:4).

Seal us up to eternal life (D&C 132:7).

The Holy Ghost also helps us prepare for the coming of the Lord. In the parable of the ten virgins, the foolish virgins were those who did not have enough oil in their lamps. To Joseph Smith, the Lord declared what the oil symbolized: "And at that day, when I shall come in my glory, shall the parable be fulfilled which I spake concerning the ten virgins. For they that are wise and have received the truth, and have taken the Holy Spirit for their guide, and have not been deceived—verily I say unto you, they shall not be hewn down and cast into the fire, but shall abide the day" (D&C 45:56–57).

The Holy Ghost is the best friend and the best guardian we could possibly have. "Now I have always said," Wilford Woodruff taught, "and I want to say it to you, that the Holy Ghost is what every Saint of God needs. It is far more important that a man should have that gift than he should have the ministration of an angel."[27] President Joseph Fielding Smith similarly stated, "We have often heard of guardian angels attending us. . . . There are times no doubt when some unseen power directs us and leads us from harm. However, the true guardian angel given to every man who comes into the world is the Light of Truth or Spirit of Christ. The Holy Ghost is given to faithful members of the Church to guard and direct them; theirs is the privilege, through their faithfulness, to have such guidance and protection."[28]

The Gift of the Holy Ghost

The gift of the Holy Ghost is different from the Holy Ghost himself. Confusion comes from failing to separate his person from his powers.[29] The gift confers upon a person the right, based on righteousness, to the constant companionship or influence of the Holy Ghost. Those who are baptized and who receive the gift of the Holy Ghost by the laying on of hands by one holding the proper priesthood authority have what President Brigham Young called "increased rays of . . . light,"[30] or as President Charles W. Penrose described, "a greater and higher endowment of the same spirit [the light of Christ] which enlightens every man that comes into the world."[31] The gift of the Holy Ghost is "the right to receive at any time, when [a person] is worthy of it and desires it, the power and light of truth of the Holy Ghost."[32] What an incredible gift! In an interview with Martin Van Buren, president of the United States, Joseph Smith was asked "wherein we differed in our religion from the other religions of the day. Brother Joseph said we differed in mode of baptism, and the gift of the Holy Ghost by the laying on of hands. We considered that all other considerations were contained in the gift of the Holy Ghost."[33]

This gift gives a person the *right*—or entitles that person to the privilege—to receive at any time when he or she is worthy of it and desires it "the power and light of truth of the Holy Ghost, although he may often be left to his own spirit and judgment."[34] There is, however, a great difference between receiving the *right* and receiving the *gift*. It is one thing to have the *right* to receive the Spirit, and another to enjoy or possess the *gift*. From the moment we are confirmed members of the Church and hear the words "Receive the Holy Ghost," we have that right, that privilege (D&C 33:15). It then becomes our responsibility to live so that we are worthy to receive the promised gift, which is opened through faith, humility, and personal righteousness.

Baptism and confirmation without receiving the Spirit are incomplete. The Prophet Joseph Smith declared, "You might as well baptize a bag of sand as a man, if not done in view of the remission of sins and getting of the Holy Ghost. Baptism by water is but half a baptism, and is good for nothing without the other half—that is, the baptism of the Holy Ghost."[35] Elder Marion G. Romney noted that "it is the mission of the Holy Ghost to reveal the truth of heaven to those who qualify to receive it. Every one of us, if we will, may so qualify. We must ever keep in mind, however, that he will not dwell in an unholy environment. He is used to the society of God, for he is an associate of the Father and the Son. When we receive the gift of the Holy Ghost, we are commanded to receive him; he is not commanded to come to us. But if, with all our hearts, we truly seek him, he will come to us and guide us in the making of decisions at every crisis of our lives."[36]

President Joseph Fielding Smith described how great the responsibility, how awesome the privilege, and how much effort is required to live so as to receive the blessings promised at baptism and confirmation: "We have a great many members of this Church who have never reached a manifestation through the Holy Ghost. Why? Because they have not made their lives conform to the truth. . . . The Holy Ghost will not dwell with that person who is unwilling to obey and keep the commandments of God or who violates those commandments willfully. In such a soul the spirit of the Holy Ghost cannot enter.

"That great gift comes to us only through humility and faith and obedience. . . .

"When we are disobedient, when our minds are set upon the things of this world rather than on the things of the kingdom of God, we cannot have the manifestations of the Holy Ghost. Did you ever stop to think what a great privilege it is for us to have the companionship of one of the members of the Godhead? Have you thought of it that way? That is our privilege, if we keep the commandments the Lord has given us."[37]

Before baptism a person may receive limited ministrations by the

Holy Ghost without the gift. The power of the Holy Ghost can come upon a person and witness that the gospel is true. These initial manifestations of truth can be given to every earnest seeker after truth.[38] But, as the Prophet Joseph Smith explained, there is a difference between experiencing such a witness and possessing the gift of the Holy Ghost: "Cornelius received the Holy Ghost before he was baptized, which was the convincing power of God unto him of the truth of the Gospel, but he could not receive the gift of the Holy Ghost until after he was baptized. Had he not taken this sign or ordinance upon him [meaning baptism and confirmation], the Holy Ghost which convinced him of the truth of God, would have left him."[39]

The receipt of the Holy Ghost after baptism is spoken of in the scriptures as a "baptism of fire" (2 Nephi 31:13), a metaphor describing the power of the Spirit to purge impurity from our souls as though burning it away by fire. A person can receive intelligence by revelation, but there is a difference between that and having our souls cleansed and sanctified. The Holy Ghost is a sanctifier who cleanses and purifies. To be born again is to be sanctified by the Holy Ghost. President Marion G. Romney explained that "one is born again by actually receiving and experiencing the light and power inherent in the gift of the Holy Ghost."[40] By being baptized and keeping the commandments, we witness to the Father that we are keeping our part of the covenant. By the baptism of fire and of the Holy Ghost, the Father and the Son witness that the covenant is in force (Ephesians 1:12–14).

President John Taylor reminded the Saints that the gift of the Holy Ghost must be cultivated and nurtured: "Now I will tell you a piece of instruction that Joseph Smith once gave me. . . . Said he, 'Elder Taylor, you have received the Holy Ghost: now follow the leadings of that spirit; and if you do, by-and-by it will become in you a principle of revelation that you will know all things as they come along and understand what is right and what is wrong in relation to them.' That is just as applicable to you if you can receive it and live up to it and enjoy it."[41]

Obedience to God's commandments places our spirits in tune with God's. By receiving the gift of the Holy Ghost, our desire to do good is increased, our motives become more refined and pure, and a deep hunger and abiding thirst for righteousness settles in. "If there is anything virtuous, lovely, or of good report or praiseworthy, we seek after these things" (Article of Faith 13). To those who receive the gift of the Holy Ghost, the Lord has promised, "The Holy Ghost shall be thy constant companion, and thy scepter an unchanging scepter of righteousness and truth" (D&C 121:46).

The gift of the Holy Ghost accelerates our spiritual growth. Elder Parley P. Pratt described how this gift helps us to become more like God: "An intelligent being, in the image of God, possesses every organ, attribute, sense, sympathy, affection, that is possessed by God himself. But these are possessed by man, in his rudimental state, in a subordinate sense of the word. Or, in other words, these attributes are in embryo, and are to be gradually developed. They resemble a bud, a germ, which gradually develops into bloom, and then, by progress, produces the mature fruit after its own kind.

"The gift of the Holy Ghost adapts itself to all these organs or attributes. It quickens all the intellectual faculties, increases, enlarges, expands, and purifies all the natural passions and affections, and adapts them, by the gift of wisdom, to their lawful use. It inspires, develops, cultivates and matures all the fine toned sympathies, joys, tastes, kindred feelings, and affections of our nature. It inspires virtue, kindness, goodness, tenderness, gentleness and charity. It develops beauty of person, form and features. It tends to health, vigor, animation and social feeling. It invigorates all the faculties of the physical and intellectual man. It strengthens and gives tone to the nerves. In short, it is, as it were, marrow to the bone, joy to the heart, light to the eyes, music to the ears, and life to the whole being."[42]

We live in what has been called a culture of disbelief, a day filled with doubt about spiritual things. This spiritual blindness comes by shortsightedness—failing to recognize truth (John 9:39), including failing to recognize God's hand in our lives. But contrary to the world's near-sighted view of the influence of the Spirit, Joseph Smith solemnly declared: "We believe in the gift of the Holy Ghost being enjoyed now, as much as it was in the Apostles' days. . . . We also believe in [the gifts of the Spirit]; and that these things cannot be enjoyed without the gift of the Holy Ghost. We believe that the holy men of old spake as they were moved by the Holy Ghost, and that holy men in these days speak by the same principle. . . . We believe that 'no man can know that Jesus is the Christ, but by the Holy Ghost.' We believe in it [this gift of the Holy Ghost] in all its fullness, and power, and greatness, and glory; but whilst we do this, we believe in it rationally, consistently, and scripturally, and not according to the wild vagaries, foolish notions and traditions of men."[43]

The Gifts of the Spirit

The gifts of the Spirit are different and distinct from the gift of the Holy Ghost. The Holy Ghost is the agent that makes all spiritual gifts available and administers them through the instrument of the light of Christ. More will be said about spiritual gifts in Chapter 8.

The Holy Spirit of Promise

The Holy Spirit of Promise is the greatest manifestation of the Spirit that can be experienced. It is the final assurance that one has obtained eternal life and stands approved before God. The Holy Spirit of Promise is the Holy Ghost. To receive the Holy Spirit of Promise is eventually to receive an ultimate assurance that was promised at the time of baptism. The phrase "receive the Holy Ghost" is an injunction to live so that the Holy Ghost will one day ratify, or approve, our righteous acts so that they will be binding on earth and in heaven. The title Holy Spirit of Promise describes the sealing and ratifying power of the Holy Ghost, "who places the stamp of approval upon every ordinance: baptism, confirmation, ordination, marriage. The promise is that the blessings will be received through faithfulness. If a person violates a covenant, whether it be of baptism, ordination, marriage or anything else, the Spirit withdraws the stamp of approval, and the blessings will not be received."[44] Thus, seals are placed on the covenants and ordinances we enter into and keep through righteousness.

The "more sure word of prophecy," as Peter referred to it (2 Peter 1:19), comes when a person follows the light of Christ God planted in his or her soul (D&C 93:31–32), hungers and thirsts after righteousness, is given a testimony by the Holy Ghost (1 Corinthians 12:3; Moroni 10:3–5), enters into covenants with God through baptism, is given the gift of the Holy Ghost by the laying on of hands, and is then taught, reproved, and guided to the baptism of fire (Matthew 3:11). The candidate continues to exercise humility and to live by every word of God (2 Nephi 31:18–21). Eventually the Lord grants the desired blessing—eternal life, which is the greatest of all the gifts of God.

This spiritual cleansing is the process of true conversion. It requires repentance, which leads to being "born of God" (Mosiah 27:25), being "quickened in the inner man" (Moses 6:65), putting off the natural man (Mosiah 3:19), experiencing a regeneration of spirit (Moses 6:59–60), being "born again" (John 3:3), being "born of the Spirit" (Mosiah 27:24), experiencing a mighty change of heart (Alma 5:14), and losing all desire for sin (JST 1 John 3:6–9; 1 John 5:18). It is accompanied by indicators that real change is taking place: peace of conscience, joy, patience, submissiveness to God's will (Mosiah 5:2), change of nature, the desire to do right always, greater spiritual enlightenment, increased commitment to covenants. It enables an individual to receive Christ's image in his or her countenance (Alma 5:14).

Elder Bruce R. McConkie taught: "Those who have been true and faithful in this life will not fall by the wayside in the life to come. If they keep their covenants here and now and depart this life firm and true in the testimony of our blessed Lord, they shall come forth with an inheritance of eternal life. We do not mean to say that those who die in the Lord, and who are true and faithful in this life, must be perfect in all things when they go into the next sphere of existence. There was only one perfect man—the Lord Jesus whose Father was God. . . . There are many things they will do and must do, even beyond the grave, to merit the fulness of the Father's kingdom in that final glorious day when the great King shall say unto them, 'Come, ye blessed of my Father, inherit the kingdom prepared for you from the foundation of the world.' (Matt. 25:34.) . . . Eventually they shall be perfect as God their Father and Christ His Son are perfect."[45]

Our spiritual growth comes a little at a time, line upon line, until the perfect day. The incredible thing is that this perfect assurance of eternal life is possible to attain: "That which is of God is light; and he that receiveth light, and continueth in God, receiveth more light; and that light groweth brighter and brighter until the perfect day" (D&C 50:24). Mortal life has been designed as the proving ground in which we are free to choose eternal life. And God has promised to give us help: "For he [God] will give unto the faithful line upon line, precept upon precept; and I will try you and prove you herewith . . . for I have decreed in my heart, saith the Lord, that I will prove you in all things, whether you will abide in my covenant, even unto death, that you may be found worthy" (D&C 98:12, 14).

If we are willing to abide in the covenants we have made with God, then we will be worthy of him, worthy to receive all the blessings he has to offer (D&C 98:15). "If thou wilt do good, yea, and hold out faithful to the end, thou shalt be saved in the kingdom of God, which is the greatest of all the gifts of God; for there is no gift greater than the gift of salvation" (D&C 6:13). "And, if you keep my commandments and endure to the end you shall have eternal life, which gift is the greatest of all the gifts of God" (D&C 14:7). Our responsibility, then, is to order our lives so that we can receive the impressions of the Spirit and be led by its influence.

Losing the Light

Joseph Smith taught, "We cannot keep all the commandments without first knowing them, and we cannot expect to know all, or more than we now know unless we comply with or keep those we have already received."[46] We can get more light by heeding what we know. Or we can lose light by rejecting what we have already received. God desires to give us revelation. He commands us to ask, knock, and seek. But he warns us that we can lose light by simply choosing not to seek or by failing to act on the inspiration that is sent (Alma 12:9–10). As President Boyd K. Packer taught, the spirit of revelation "is awakened with prayer and cultivated 'by obedience to the laws and ordinances of the Gospel.' (Article of Faith 1:3.) It can be smothered through transgression and neglect."[47]

Anciently, Isaiah taught that the light within will guide us through life and will whisper to us: "And thine ears shall hear a word behind thee, saying, This is the way, walk ye in it, when ye turn to the right hand, and when ye turn to the left" (Isaiah 30:21). He also warned that to ignore the light within and to try to go through life using only our own reasoning and judgment would be foolish in the extreme: "Behold, all ye that kindle a fire, that compass yourselves about with sparks: walk in the light of your fire, and in the sparks that ye have kindled. This shall ye have of mine hand; ye shall lie down in sorrow" (Isaiah 50:11).

The light within can be strengthened. The Prophet Joseph Smith taught that "all the minds and spirits that God ever sent into the world are susceptible of enlargement."[48] We can receive as much light as we are willing to receive and grow from grace to grace (D&C 93:12–13). The Lord pours out his Spirit on those with a "willingness to believe in his words" (Helaman 6:36).

Yet the light can also be lost. If an individual turns away from the light, he or she will begin to deny revelation from the Holy Spirit. Anything that offends the Spirit is sin, and sin causes the Holy Ghost to withdraw. The light of Christ will stay with us for a long time, but the Holy Ghost will not strive, or struggle, with us. When we offend the Holy Ghost, he leaves. The light of Christ "strives" to keep us in the light, but if we "strive" (contend) against the Holy Ghost, he departs.

There is a difference between the Holy Ghost withdrawing because of sin and withdrawing of his own accord: "My Spirit shall not always strive with man," the Lord has said (D&C 1:33). There are times when we are left to our own best judgment. That is part of the test of mortality.

Throughout history, individuals following the Spirit have led society to enlightenment and discovery. Losing the Spirit has always led to cultural and intellectual degeneracy.[49] King Benjamin reminded his people of the blessings that flow from obedience to the light: "And moreover, I would desire that ye should consider on the blessed and happy state of those that keep the commandments of God. For behold, they are blessed in all things, both temporal and spiritual; and if they hold out faithful to the end they are received into heaven, that thereby they may dwell with God in a state of never-ending happiness. O remember, remember that these things are true; for the Lord God hath spoken it" (Mosiah 2:41).

The prophet Alma reminded his people that the light within can be brightened or dimmed: "He that will harden his heart, the same receiveth the lesser portion of the word; and he that will not harden his heart, to him is given the greater portion of the word, until it is given unto him to know the mysteries of God until he know them in full. And they that will harden their hearts, to them is given the lesser portion of the word until they know nothing concerning his mysteries; and then they are taken captive by the devil, and led by his will down to destruction. Now this is what is meant by the chains of hell" (Alma 12:10–11).

If the light within is dimmed by unrighteousness, for example, we lose not only civility and truth but life itself. We cannot live without light from heaven: "When the Spirit ceaseth to strive with man then cometh speedy destruction" (2 Nephi 26:11). When the Nephites were fully ripened in iniquity, they were destroyed. As Brigham Young explained, "In every man is a candle of the Lord which burns with a clear light; and if by the wickedness of a man it is extinguished, then farewell for ever to that individual."[50]

Without the light within, there is nothing left to impel men to do good. Mormon's lament for his people was for this type of spiritual depravity: "For behold, the Spirit of the Lord hath already ceased to strive with [them]; and they are without Christ and God in the world; and they are driven about as chaff before the wind. They were once a delightsome people, and they had Christ for their shepherd; yea, they were led even by God the Father. But now, behold, they are led about by Satan, even as . . . a vessel is tossed about upon the waves, without sail or anchor, or without anything wherewith to steer her" (Mormon 5:16–18).

Elder Neal A. Maxwell has observed that societies which are all sail and no anchor—societies that permit anything—soon lose everything.[51] The adversary is a deceiver who causes us to drift away from principles and anchors. When people are deceived, their personal righteousness is lessened.

Individuals who turn away from the light persecute the truth. When Isaac Behunnin heard the Prophet Joseph describe how badly he had been treated by apostates who were once close to the faith, he remarked, "If I should leave this Church, I would not do as those men have done. I would go to some remote place where Mormonism had never been heard of, and no one would ever learn that I knew anything about it." The great Seer immediately replied: "Brother Behunnin, you don't know what you would do. No doubt these men once thought as you do. Before you joined this Church you stood on neutral ground. When the gospel was preached, good and evil were set before you. You could choose either or neither. There were two opposite masters inviting you to serve them. When you joined this Church you enlisted to serve God. When you did that, you left the neutral ground, and you never can get back on it. Should you forsake the Master you enlisted to serve, it will be by the instigation of the evil one, and you will follow his dictation and be his servant."[52]

In the Book of Mormon we see whole societies rise and fall dramatically in just a few years (Alma 1–4; Helaman 1–5). The Spirit withdraws because of their wickedness and the hardness of their hearts (Helaman 5:35). Without the Spirit they become "hardened and impenitent and grossly wicked" (Helaman 6:2). Such people begin to depend "upon their own strength and upon their own wisdom" (Helaman 16:15). Satan stirs "them up to do iniquity continually" (Helaman 16:22), and they begin to live "without principle" (Moroni 9:20). The Lord withholds his Spirit (D&C 64:16), and they become, as Paul described, past feeling, having "given themselves over unto lasciviousness, to work all uncleanness with greediness" (Ephesians 4:19). When men love Satan more than they love God, they begin "from that time forth to be carnal, sensual, and devilish" (Moses 5:13). At one point in their degeneracy, the Nephites had even become more "wild, wicked and ferocious" than their enemies (Alma 47:36). That is why the Lord calls on his children "by the Holy Ghost everywhere and command[s] them that they should repent; and as many as [believe] in the Son, and [repent] of their sins, should be saved; and as many as [believe] not and [repent] not, should be damned" (Moses 5:14–15).

The Prophet Joseph Smith described why sinning against revelation from the Holy Ghost is so serious: "All sins shall be forgiven, except the sin against the Holy Ghost; for Jesus will save all except the sons of perdition. What must a man do to commit the unpardonable sin? He must receive the Holy Ghost, have the heavens opened unto him, and know God, and then sin against Him. After a man has sinned against the Holy Ghost, there is no repentance for him. He has got to say that the sun does not shine while he sees it; he has got to deny Jesus Christ when the heavens have been opened unto him, and to deny the plan of salvation with his eyes open to the truth of it; and from that time he begins to be an enemy. This is the case with many apostates of the Church of Jesus Christ of Latter-day Saints.

"When a man begins to be an enemy to this work, he hunts me, he seeks to kill me, and never ceases to thirst for my blood. He gets the spirit of the devil—the same spirit that they had who crucified the Lord of Life—the same spirit that sins against the Holy Ghost. You cannot save such persons; you cannot bring them to repentance; they make open war, like the devil, and awful is the consequence. . . .

"There have been remarks made concerning all men being redeemed from hell; but I say that those who sin against the Holy Ghost cannot be forgiven in this world or in the world to come; they shall die the second death."[53]

Message of Hope

As foreboding as the warnings are, there is a grand and glorious promise from God that we should cling to: Regardless of how far away from the light we have strayed, God still invites us to return (Ether 9:34–35). The door is always open: "Behold, he sendeth an invitation unto all men, for the arms of mercy are extended towards them, and he saith: Repent, and I will receive you" (Alma 5:33). We can rekindle the light within our souls, even in our darkest moments. Even Korihor, the anti-Christ who fought against the Church and denied God, exclaimed at the end of his perverse life, "I always knew that there was a God" (Alma 30:52).

President J. Reuben Clark Jr. said: "Every human being is born with the light of faith kindled in his heart as on an altar, and that light burns and the Lord sees that it burns, during the period before we are accountable. When accountability comes then each of us determines how we shall feed and care for that light. If we shall live righteously that light will glow until it suffuses the whole body, giving to it health and strength and spiritual light as well as bodily health. If we shall live unrighteously that light will dwindle and finally almost flicker out. Yet it is my hope and my belief that *the Lord never permits the light of faith wholly to be extinguished* in any human heart, however faint the light may glow. The Lord has provided that there shall still be there a spark which, with teaching, with the spirit of righteousness, with love, with tenderness, with example, with living the Gospel, shall brighten and glow again, however darkened the mind may have been. And if we shall fail so to reach those among us of our own whose faith has dwindled low, we shall fail in one of the main things which the Lord expects at our hands."[55]

God has given us many great gifts: the gift of a mind with which to think; the gift of a soul with which to feel; the gift of the Holy Ghost with which to know; and the gift of revelation (the light within) that connects all these gifts. What could be more important in life than putting ourselves in tune with the Spirit of God? We cannot comprehend all things, but God does (D&C 88:41). He has promised those who seek his Spirit that "the day shall come when [they] shall comprehend even God, being quickened in him and by him" (D&C 88:49). The light within, revelation from heaven in all its forms, is the key to knowing God and finding eternal life (Alma 38:6). As Elder Neal A. Maxwell said: "Little wonder that weekly, when we partake of the sacramental bread, we ask to have the Spirit *always* with us. Only then are we safe. Otherwise, without the Spirit, we are left to ourselves. Who would ever want to solo anyway?"[56]

Notes

1. McConkie, *New Witness*, 257.
2. Smith, *Doctrines of Salvation*, 1:51.
3. *Children's Songbook*, 177.
4. Ehat and Cook, *Words of Joseph Smith*, 64, 245, 382; Cannon, Dahl, and Welch, "The Restoration of Major Doctrines through Joseph Smith," 29.
5. McConkie, *Mormon Doctrine*, 359.
6. Smith, *Teachings*, 275–76.
7. Smith, *Doctrines of Salvation*, 1:40.
8. Smith, *Doctrines of Salvation*, 1:55.
9. Talmage, *Articles of Faith*, 160.
10. Young, *Journal of Discourses*, 6:95; see also John 16:13–14.
11. Lee, *Decisions for Successful Living*, 144.
12. "Preparing for influence of Holy Ghost," 7.
13. Smith, *Teachings*, 190.
14. Pratt, *Key to the Science of Theology*, 45; see also Alma 26:22; Jacob 4:8.
15. Smith, *Teachings*, 328.
16. Smith, *Doctrines of Salvation*, 1:47–48.
17. McConkie, *Here We Stand*, 194.
18. Smith, *Teachings*, 160.
19. Young, *Journal of Discourses*, 9:254.
20. Smith, *Gospel Doctrine*, 13–14.
21. Pratt, *Series of Pamphlets*, 57.
22. McConkie, *Doctrinal New Testament Commentary*, 3:386.
23. Smith, *Teachings*, 324.
24. Eyring, Conference Report, April 1996, 84–85.
25. "Preparing for influence of Holy Ghost," 7.
26. Smith, *Doctrines of Salvation*, 1:41.
27. Woodruff, *Deseret Weekly* 53 (7 November 1896): 641.
28. Smith, *Doctrines of Salvation*, 1:54.
29. Talmage, *Articles of Faith*, 160.
30. Young, *Journal of Discourses*, 6:315.
31. Penrose, *Journal of Discourses*, 23:350.
32. Smith, *Gospel Doctrine*, 61.
33. Smith, *History of the Church*, 4:42.
34. Smith, *Gospel Doctrine*, 61.
35. Smith, *Teachings*, 314.
36. Romney, "Revelation in Our Personal Affairs," 647.
37. Smith, "Fundamental Gospel Truths," 14.
38. Smith, *Answers to Gospel Questions*, 3:29.
39. Smith, *Teachings*, 199.
40. Romney, Conference Report, April 1977, 61.

41. Taylor, *Journal of Discourses*, 20:227.
42. Pratt, *Key to the Science of Theology*, 61–62.
43. Smith, *Teachings*, 243.
44. Smith, *Doctrines of Salvation*, 1:45.
45. McConkie, *Ensign*, November 1976, 107.
46. Smith, *Teachings*, 256.
47. Packer, *Ensign*, May 2000, 9.
48. Smith, *Teachings*, 354.
49. Smith, *Progress of Man*, 199–200.
50. Young, *Journal of Discourses*, 9:104.
51. Maxwell, *Ensign*, May 1995, 67.
52. Reported by Daniel Tyler, *Juvenile Instructor,* as cited in Andrus and Andrus, *They Knew the Prophet*, 60–61.
53. Smith, *Teachings*, 358, 361.
54. Clark, Conference Report, October 1936, 114; emphasis added.
55. Maxwell, "Teaching by the Spirit," 3.

Chapter 3

Light for the Journey Home

After the death of Joseph Smith, President Brigham Young had a dream in which the Prophet visited him and gave him a message: "Joseph stepped toward me, and looking very earnestly, yet pleasantly, said: 'Tell the people to be humble and faithful, and be sure to keep the spirit of the Lord and it will lead them right. Be careful and not turn away the small still voice; it will teach them what to do and where to go. . . . Tell the brethren to keep their hearts open to conviction, so that when the Holy Ghost comes to them their hearts will be ready to receive it. . . . Tell the brethren if they will follow the spirit of the Lord they will go right. Be sure to tell the people to keep the spirit of the Lord.'"[1]

Later President Wilford Woodruff said that Brigham Young had also visited him after his death and delivered the same message he had received from Joseph. Brigham Young had told him: "I want you to teach the people to get the Spirit of God. You cannot build up the Kingdom of God without that."[2] It is the Spirit that matters most. Revelation, Joseph Smith taught, is "the most glorious principle of the Gospel of Jesus Christ."[3] Revelation is "the key that unlocks the heavens and puts in our possession the glories of the celestial world."[4] Having the Spirit is so important that each week at the sacrament table God renews his promise to us that we "may always have his Spirit to be with [us]" if we keep his commandments and remember his Son (D&C 20:77, 79). That promise and its weekly renewal is a supernal privilege.

The Prophet Joseph has warned the Saints that "nothing is a greater injury to the children of men than to be under the influence of a false spirit when they think they have the Spirit of God."[5] The ability to discern between the Spirit of God and other spirits, especially pseudospiritual experiences that seek to imitate God's Spirit, will prove even more important as we approach the second coming of the Lord (D&C 45:56–57). Life may be physically easier today than in other dispensations, but confrontation with the evil one is greater than it has been in a long time. We can be blessed to be equal to the times in which we live.

The only way not to be deceived is to have the Holy Ghost. The Prophet Joseph taught, "Unless some person or persons have a communication, or revelation from God, unfolding to them the operation of the spirit, they must eternally remain ignorant."[6] If we ever lose the Holy Ghost, we will fail. It is of critical importance to obtain that Spirit, to prepare our minds to receive its promptings, and to carry its influence with us through life. Joseph Smith expressed his confidence in the Spirit when he said, "I am learned, and know more than all the world put together. The Holy Ghost does, anyhow, and He . . . comprehends more than all the world: and I will associate myself with Him."[7]

In the Presence of the Divine

We are always in the presence of the Divine, but at some point in life, we all probably wonder about our relationship to God. President David O. McKay wisely observed that there are moments when we deeply and sincerely desire the high road, spiritually speaking: "Man is a spiritual being, a soul, and at some period of his life everyone is possessed with an irresistible desire to know his relationship to the Infinite. . . . There is something within him which urges him to rise above himself, to control his environment, to master the body and all things physical and live in a higher and more beautiful world."[8]

We all want to discover our calling in life, our life's mission. That is why the "development of our spiritual nature should concern us most. Spirituality is the highest acquisition of the soul, the divine in man; 'the supreme, crowning gift that makes him king of all created things.' It is the consciousness of victory over self and of communion with the Infinite. It is spirituality alone which really gives one the best in life."[9]

Everything about mortality's temporal (temporary) nature tells us that this earth is not our permanent home. In the eternal perspective, mortal life is like being sent off for a day at school. In our premortal existence, when it was announced that the earth was finished and that we could begin our mortal probation, we shouted for joy (Job 38:4–7). But now that we are here, there are days when "we wonder what all the shouting was about."[10] Life is very challenging, but there is an equality to the trials and tests we face. All too soon, however, our day at school ends. The bell rings, and we all go home.

The meaning of life and the purpose for our existence can only be known by revelation. Indeed, God has revealed many important truths regarding the purpose of life. The Prophet Joseph observed: "It is important that we should understand the reasons and causes of our exposure to the vicissitudes of life and of death, and the designs and purposes of God in our coming into the world, our sufferings here, and our departure hence. What is the object of our coming into existence, then dying and falling away, to be here no more? It is but reasonable to suppose that God would reveal something in reference to the matter, and it is a subject we ought to study more than any other. We ought to study it day and night, for the world is ignorant in reference to their true condition and relation. If we have any claim on our Heavenly Father for anything, it is for knowledge on this important subject."[11]

Balanced by the Spirit

Because we are here on earth for divine purposes, one great challenge of mortality is not to be distracted or deflected from doing the things that matter most. Satan desires to "distract us from our heritage," Elder Marvin J. Ashton taught, but "our eternal home is our ultimate destination. A proper yearning for home can prevent our getting lost in detours or paths that lead us away." Satan is delighted when we are overly involved in things that are not important in the eternal scheme. "He'd like to keep us so busy with comparatively insignificant things that we don't have time to make the effort to understand where we came from, whose children we are, and how glorious our ultimate homecoming can be!"[12] We must always remember who we are and Whose we are.

The Holy Ghost helps us keep all things in proper perspective. The Holy Ghost keeps us in balance. Like a tightrope walker, if we overdo principles of the gospel, or if we under-do certain things, we can fall. Our Heavenly Father is anxious to send revelation to guide and balance us along our journey through mortality.

Personal Initiative

As the "Father of lights" (D&C 67:9), our Heavenly Father can send us light for our journey, just as he did for the Jaredites: "And thus the Lord caused stones to shine in darkness, to give light unto men, women, and children, that they might not cross the great waters in darkness" (Ether 6:3).

But God never reveals so much that our moral agency is stifled. Nor does he overwhelm us with details that crush personal initiative. His plan provides the opportunity for us to work under the influence of the Spirit, but he expects us to act and choose for ourselves. "Men should be anxiously engaged in a good cause, and do many things of their own free will, and bring to pass much righteousness; for the power is in them, wherein they are agents unto themselves" (D&C 58:27–28).

Although sometimes we may feel that our temporal affairs are of no concern to God, where we live, when and where we move, and whom we befriend are all things that can affect our journey home. Does God care about how we journey through life? About which paths we choose as we attempt to return home? Absolutely. God is as concerned with where we end up in the next life as he is with how we get there. We might ask ourselves, Do we care as much? When the Saints were moving from Kirtland, Ohio, to Far West, Missouri, in 1838, Hyrum Smith observed that their attempts at organizing themselves were not very successful. He pondered about why their journey was so difficult and realized that he had made plans "according to his own judgment without reference to the testimony of the Spirit of God" and that the "Saints had to act oftentimes upon their own responsibility without any reference to the testimony of the Spirit of God in relation to temporal affairs."[13]

Need for Spiritual Enlightenment

With the huge changes that occur so quickly in society and with the numerous unforeseen events that affect our distinct and diverse journeys through life, we have an innate need for light and revelation from a higher power. Joseph Smith underscored that need for revelation when he stated that "we are differently situated from any other people that ever existed upon this earth; consequently those former revelations [in the scriptures] cannot be suited to our conditions; they were given to other people, who were before us."[14]

Without inspiration from heaven, we risk making serious mistakes in judgment that could have eternal consequences. We need revelation, and it is not unreasonable, nor is it unscriptural, to expect it. The Prophet Joseph said, "This is the principle on which the government of heaven is conducted—by revelation adapted to the circumstances in which the children of the kingdom are placed."[15] Like the prophet Nephi, those who desire to "see, and hear, and know of these things, by the power of the Holy Ghost," will receive that gift. It is given "unto all those who diligently seek him. . . . For he is the same yesterday, to-day, and forever; and the way is prepared for all. . . . For he that diligently seeketh shall find; and the mysteries of God shall be unfolded unto them, by the power of the Holy Ghost, as well in these times as in times of old, and as well in times of old as in times to come" (1 Nephi 10:17–19).

We can count on God to keep his promises. "Our God can be

trusted to the very uttermost. No matter how serious the trial, how deep the distress, how great the affliction, He will never desert us. He never has, and He never will. He cannot do it. It is not His character. He is an unchangeable being; the same yesterday, the same today, and He will be the same throughout the eternal ages to come. We have found that God. We have made Him our friend, by obeying His Gospel; and He will stand by us."[16] Because God always keeps his promises, the "crucial test of our lives" is to see "if we will make and keep our covenants with Him."[17]

Accomplishing Our Purpose

Life is an adventurous journey with both high and low moments. The light within is a sure guide that will lead us home. The Lord doesn't spell out every step because we are here to learn and grow and explore, but he has not left us in the dark, either. President Ezra Taft Benson said, "Usually the Lord gives us the overall objectives to be accomplished and some guidelines to follow, but he expects us to work out most of the details and methods. The methods and procedures are usually developed through study and prayer and by living so that we can obtain and follow the promptings of the Spirit. Less spiritually advanced people, such as those in the days of Moses, had to be commanded in many things. Today those spiritually alert look at the objectives, check the guidelines laid down by the Lord and his prophets, and then prayerfully act—without having to be commanded 'in all things.' This attitude prepares men for godhood."[18]

We need to learn, as Brigham Young put it, to be "righteous in the dark."[19] Without the Spirit we are in danger of being lost. We have many trials and tribulations to pass through, but we also have a high destiny. If we develop our individual capacities and wisely exercise our agency, God will help us to become "illuminated individuals," to radiate a "gospel glow," and help us be of good cheer—even "amid dark difficulties."[20]

A great example of one who trusted in God and who moved

forward in life despite overwhelming obstacles is the prophet Nephi. When he was commanded to build a ship sturdy enough to carry a large group of people across the ocean to the promised land, he had to work it out in his mind, plan carefully, ponder for periods of time, and seek for inspiration. The Lord gave the "overall objectives . . . and some guidelines to follow," just as President Benson explained, but it was up to Nephi to seek inspiration and to use his own ingenuity and ideas. The Lord reassured him: "I will be your light . . . and I will prepare the way before you, if it so be that ye shall keep my commandments; . . . and ye shall know that it is by me that ye are led" (1 Nephi 17:13). Nephi described his experience with these words:

"And it came to pass that the Lord spake unto me, saying: Thou shalt construct a ship, after the manner which I shall show thee, that I may carry thy people across these waters. . . .

"And it came to pass that they did worship the Lord, and did go forth with me; and we did work timbers of curious workmanship. And the Lord did show me from time to time after what manner I should work the timbers of the ship.

"Now I, Nephi, did not work the timbers after the manner which was learned by men, neither did I build the ship after the manner of men; but I did build it after the manner which the Lord had shown unto me; wherefore, it was not after the manner of men.

"And I, Nephi, did go into the mount oft, and I did pray oft unto the Lord; wherefore the Lord showed unto me great things.

"And it came to pass that after I had finished the ship, according to the word of the Lord, my brethren beheld that it was good, and that the workmanship thereof was exceedingly fine" (1 Nephi 17:8; 18:1–4).

Reread Nephi's account and substitute words that are meaningful to you regarding your purpose in life. Perhaps replace the words *ship* and *timbers* with *family* and *children*. Or replace them with *career* and *job*, or *education* and *skills*. We can "go to the mount oft" and have God show us "from time to time" what to do and how to proceed. By following Nephi's example, we will one day be able to look back on our efforts and accomplishments and realize that with God's help, they were "good" and "exceedingly fine"—even better than we could have ever done on our own.

President Ezra Taft Benson promised: "Men and women who turn their lives over to God will discover that He can make a lot more out of their lives than they can. He will deepen their joys, expand their vision, quicken their minds, strengthen their muscles, lift their spirits, multiply their blessings, increase their opportunities, comfort their souls, raise up friends, and pour out peace."[21] Which of these blessings do we need most? We can receive it!

We each have a purpose in life. God can help us accomplish our foreknown and foreordained role, just as he helped Nephi. And he is pleased to do so. Our Heavenly Father has invited and wants us to have a close relationship with him: "Draw near unto me and I will draw near unto you; seek me diligently and ye shall find me; ask, and ye shall receive; knock, and it shall be opened unto you" (D&C 88:63).

Just as he led the children of Israel through the wilderness with a pillar of fire, so he will lead us with the Holy Ghost. Just as he guided Lehi's colony with the Liahona, so he will guide us with revelation from heaven. "The gift of the Holy Ghost is the greatest of all the gifts of God, as pertaining to this life; and those who enjoy that gift here and now, will inherit eternal life hereafter, which is the greatest of all the gifts of God in eternity."[22]

Is the Lord interested in our lives? Does he have a plan for the salvation of all his children? Is there purpose and meaning to life? Prophetic statements answer yes. And although we may not know specific details about our roles in the Savior's work to "bring to pass the immortality and eternal life of man" (Moses 1:39), the Lord has revealed to us the broad guidelines and gospel principles necessary. Elder Merrill J. Bateman has commented that God "asks his servants to seek and listen to the Spirit in order to fill in the details. For example, the charge to the First Presidency and the Quorum of the Twelve is to take the gospel to every nation, kindred, tongue, and people, but the Lord does not tell them how or when or where except through the quiet whisperings of the Spirit. The same is true for [us]. Guidelines have been given by the Lord, and it is important that all of us listen to the whisperings of the Spirit."[23] Those whisperings are like a pleasant voice speaking to our soul (Helaman 5:46, 30): "And thine ears shall hear a word behind thee, saying, This is the way, walk ye in it" (Isaiah 30:21).

Guided by the Light

Another excellent example of a group led by revelation is the Jaredites. When they were guided to their land of promise, they were well prepared by the Lord for the experience. The brother of Jared and his people equipped eight barges to carry them across the ocean to their new home. The Lord had instructed him how to construct the barges so they would have air but invited the brother of Jared to think of a way to get light into them. It was as if the Lord were saying, "I'll help you. But I want you to do some things. Then, when you are ready, I'll meet you and give you more help." Ether recounts that "the Lord said unto the brother of Jared: What will ye that I should do that ye may have light in your vessels? For behold, ye cannot have windows, for they will be dashed in pieces; neither shall ye take fire with you, for ye shall not go by the light of fire" (Ether 2:23).

The brother of Jared pondered, prayed, and worked hard to think of an idea. He fashioned sixteen molten stones that were "white and clear, even as transparent glass" and then presented them before the Lord (Ether 3:1).

He asked the Lord to touch them that they might shine in the darkness. The Lord "stretched forth his hand and touched the stones one by one with his finger" and the stones began to shine (Ether 3:6). Because of his great faith in the Lord, the brother of Jared "could not be kept from beholding within the veil [and] he could not be kept from within the veil" (Ether 3:19–20). He was privileged to see Christ, who ministered to him (Ether 3:20). God is so generous that he gives us the light and knowledge we seek after—and often much more.

The Lord helped the Jaredites prepare for their journey. He warned them about the dangers they would face (Ether 2:24) and promised, "Behold, I prepare you against these things" (Ether 2:25). Similarly, God will do the same for us. He not only prepares us to face the waves that occasionally rise up against us during our mortal sojourn, but he also calms the storms after they hit. The experience of the hand of the Lord directing the Jaredites is a type of what God has done and will do for us. Consider how the journey of the Jaredites relates to our journey through life:

"For it came to pass after the Lord had prepared the stones which the brother of Jared had carried [before Him] . . . behold, they did give light unto the vessels" (Ether 6:2). The Lord expects us to do our part—to carry before him all we are capable of doing ourselves—and ask him to touch our efforts. If we desire revelation from him, we must use our minds and hearts to think of what we should do, and make the best choices we are capable of making. To Oliver Cowdery (who wanted to translate the Book of Mormon record by the power of the Holy Ghost, as Joseph Smith had done, but who failed) the Lord said, "Behold, you have not understood; you have supposed that I would give it unto you, when you took no thought save it was to ask me. But, behold, I say unto you, that you must study it out in your mind; then you must ask me if it be right, and if it is right I will cause . . . you [to] feel that it is right" (D&C 9:7–8).

"The Lord caused stones to shine in darkness, to give light unto men, women, and children, that they might not cross the great waters in darkness" (Ether 6:3). The Lord sends revelations to all of us—men, women, and children—to help us on our journey. We have been given many "stones that shine in darkness," including patriarchal blessings, answers to humble prayers, promptings by the Holy Ghost, wise counsel from parents, inspired guidance from Church leaders and scriptures.

"They . . . prepared all manner of food, that thereby they might subsist on the water" (Ether 6:4). We come to this earth having spent many, many years preparing ourselves and being prepared by others for our experiences (D&C 138:56). We were taught many lessons and prepared by God to do these things on earth long before we were born (D&C 138:53–56). It is not coincidence that we are here now, in these latter days, carrying the message of the gospel and making temple blessings available to Heavenly Father's children all over the earth.

"And it came to pass that when they had done all these things they got aboard of their vessels or barges, and set forth into the sea, commending

themselves unto the Lord their God" (*Ether 6:4*). As we left heaven to begin life on earth, we came with great trust in God. The Jaredites' climbing into barges and beginning the journey across an uncharted ocean is much like our taking bodies and beginning mortal life. We exercised a great deal of faith in God that he would help us get through life and guide us back into his presence. We commended ourselves to his watchful care and tender mercy.

"And it came to pass that the Lord God caused that there should be a furious wind blow upon the face of the waters, towards the promised land" (*Ether 6:5*). Opposition and trials of faith, like fierce winds, blow against us all through mortality. But, as difficult as they are, they blow the chaff away and lift us to higher levels of living. They are like the wind beneath eagles wings that can help us not only fly high to where God dwells but become even as he is. Speaking of the refining he gained from his trials, the Prophet Joseph said, "I am like a huge, rough stone rolling down from a high mountain; and the only polishing I get is when some corner gets rubbed off by coming in contact with something else, . . . all hell knocking off a corner here and a corner there. Thus I will become a smooth and polished shaft in the quiver of the Almighty, who will give me dominion over all."[24]

"Thus they were tossed upon the waves of the sea before the wind. . . . They were many times buried in the depths of the sea, because of the mountain waves which broke upon them" (*Ether 6:5–6*). Life's challenges seem, quite often, to be just as overwhelming. The heartaches and the crosses we are called to bear sometimes seem about to crush us. But the Lord has promised us strength. He could step in and save us just as the waves begin to dash against us, but He knows that "all these things shall give [us] experience, and shall be for [our] good" (D&C 122:7). He could rush to our aid at the first hint of billowing surges, but he often waits until the "fourth watch" when we have learned and experienced the most: "And he saw them toiling in rowing; for the wind was contrary unto them: and about the fourth watch of the night he cometh unto them, walking upon the sea . . . [and said] Be of good cheer: it is I; be not afraid" (Mark 6:48, 50).

With God as our friend, we have no need to fear. The prophet Isaiah used many metaphors to teach Israel of God's protective strength. He said that God is our sure foundation; when we cry to him, he hears; we need not fear nor be dismayed because he will uphold and strengthen us; he will never forget us, we are engraven in the palms of his hands; God is our refuge from the storm and a shadow from the heat; he is a hiding place from the fierce winds, a covert (covering) from the tempest, like rivers of water in a dry place; and he will wipe away all tears from our eyes (Isaiah 28:16; 30:18–19; 41:10; 49:14–16; 25:4; 32:2; 25:8).

"Therefore when they were encompassed about by many waters they did cry unto the Lord, and he did bring them forth again upon the top of the waters" (Ether 6:7). Prayer unlocks the door that leads to God's help. When we "pour out [our] souls" in our secret places and let our hearts be fully "drawn out in prayer unto him continually for [our] welfare, and also for the welfare of those who are around [us]" (Alma 34:26–27) he answers and comes to help. Having faith in God means having faith he exists, that he has all power, but it also means having faith in his timing. His help is given "in his own time, and in his own way, and according to his own will" (D&C 88:68).

"And it came to pass that the wind did never cease to blow towards the promised land while they were upon the waters" (Ether 6:8). The restraints or limitations that trials place on our lives and the pain, mental anguish, or heartaches that accompany them can sometimes last throughout our entire lives. We know that God has power eventually to deliver us out of bondage and totally free us from our trials, but we know he also has great compassion and mercy for us in the midst of our suffering: "I will also ease the burdens which are put upon your shoulders, that even you cannot feel them upon your backs, even while you are in bondage; and this will I do that ye may stand as witnesses for me hereafter, and that ye may know of a surety that I, the Lord God, do visit my people in their afflictions" (Mosiah 24:14). Hence the need to "submit cheerfully and with patience to all the will of the Lord" (Mosiah 24:15).

"They did sing praises unto the Lord; yea, the brother of Jared did sing praises unto the Lord, and he did thank and praise the Lord all the day long; and when the night came, they did not cease to praise the Lord" (Ether 6:9). Gratitude for God's blessings, even the smallest ones, often has a direct

correlation to our humility and meekness. If we fail to show gratitude for small kindnesses and favors, would we have forgotten to say thanks for being healed from leprosy? Nine out of ten who were healed forgot (Luke 17:16–17). An attitude of gratitude, even before we are delivered from our trials, shows God we trust him.

"Thus they were driven forth; and no monster of the sea could break them, neither whale that could mar them; and they did have light continually, whether it was above the water or under the water" (Ether 6:10). Whether in good times or in bad, the light of revelation will continually work to protect those who put their trust in God.

"Thus they were driven forth, three hundred and forty and four days upon the water" (Ether 6:11). Three hundred and forty-four days is nearly a whole year—a long time, especially in barges. It must have felt like an eternity. Yet mortality, from an eternal perspective, is very short. While we are experiencing it, it seems like a long, long journey, but from God's eternal perspective, our mortal sojourn constitutes a very short period of separation.

"They did land upon the shore of the promised land. And when they had set their feet upon the shores of the promised land they bowed themselves down upon the face of the land, and did humble themselves before the Lord, and did shed tears of joy before the Lord, because of the multitude of his tender mercies over them" (Ether 6:12). When we return to God's glorious presence, we will probably fall down at his feet. Tears of gratitude and appreciation will surely flow freely. How awesome it will be to realize that we will lose none of the friendships we developed in life: "That same sociality which exists among us here will exist among us there, only it will be coupled with eternal glory, which glory we do not now enjoy" (D&C 130:2). President Brigham Young testified that "we talk about our trials and troubles here in this life: but suppose that you could see yourselves thousands and millions of years after you have proved faithful to your religion during the few short years in this time, and have obtained eternal salvation and a crown of glory in the presence of God; then look back upon your lives here, and see the losses, crosses, and disappointments, the sorrows . . . , you would be constrained to exclaim, 'But what of all that? Those things were but for a moment, and we are now here.'"[25]

After Joseph who was sold into Egypt was delivered from all his trials, he named his two sons Manasseh and Ephraim, to symbolize God's love and power of deliverance. *Manasseh* means "God . . . hath made me forget all my toil" and Ephraim means "God hath caused me to be fruitful in the land of my affliction" (Genesis 41:51–52). One day, like the Jaredites, we will all "shed tears of joy before the Lord, because of his multitude of tender mercies" and will all feel to exclaim, "Manasseh! Ephraim!"

Eternal Blessings—Worth Every Effort

If the storms of life were not so strong, would we be able to fully appreciate the sunny days in the celestial kingdom? If the winds were not so fierce here and now, would we be able to appreciate the calm and peace that exist in heaven? If the good and the beautiful were easily found, would we ever appreciate the transcendent beauty that will be so abundant there for us to enjoy?

Life has been designed to test each of us in highly personal ways, but it has also been designed so that we will appreciate how incredibly awesome heaven is (D&C 137). Heaven is so different from this fallen world that no mortal eye has ever seen, no mortal mind has ever conceived of anything as great as the blessings waiting for the faithful, those who love and wait patiently for the Savior to appear (1 Corinthians 2:9; D&C 133:45). How long will we go on praising God for his plan for our salvation and for the "multitude of his tender mercies"? The scriptures declare "forever and ever" (Mosiah 2:24; D&C 20:16; 65:6; 76:21, 93, 110, 119; 84:102; 88:104; JST Revelation 1:6).

President George Q. Cannon described God's blessings and rewards in these words: "We may pass through the fiery furnace; we may pass through deep waters; but we shall not be consumed nor overwhelmed. We shall emerge from all these trials and difficulties the better and purer for them, if we only trust in God and keep his commandments. Then He has a future for us. That bliss which we have a foretaste of here, we shall have a fulness of hereafter. You who have received the

Holy Spirit; you who have felt its power; you whose hearts have been gladdened under its heavenly influence, you know how sweet it has been; you know that there is nothing on earth so sweet as the outpouring of the Spirit of God on a human being. No matter what experience you may have had in riches and in all that earth desires, there is nothing that compares with the heavenly sweetness and joy of the Spirit of God. This is a foretaste of that which is to come. We shall receive a fulness of that, if we are faithful. If we hold on without flinching, and without turning to the right hand or to the left, our God will lead us straight on until we are brought into His presence and crowned with glory, immortality and eternal life; which I pray may be the happy lot of every one of us."[26]

God Comprehends Our Circumstances

Just as God blessed Nephi, just as he helped the Jaredites prepare for their journey, and just as he constantly pushed and guided them both towards the promised land, he will help us. God loves and cares for every person and family and nation that has lived or will yet live on this earth. The Prophet Joseph gave us the accounts of Nephi and of the Jaredites. Their stories in the Book of Mormon help us remember God's tender mercies are "over all those whom he hath chosen, because of their faith, to make them mighty even unto the power of deliverance" (1 Nephi 1:20; Moroni 10:3).

The Prophet Joseph testified: "The great Jehovah contemplated the whole of the events connected with the earth, pertaining to the plan of salvation, before it rolled into existence, or ever 'the morning stars sang together' for joy; the past, the present, and the future were and are, with Him, one eternal 'now;' He knew of the fall of Adam, the iniquities of the antediluvians, of the depth of iniquity that would be connected with the human family, their weakness and strength, their power and glory, apostasies, their crimes, their righteousness and iniquity; He comprehended the fall of man, and his redemption; He knew the plan of salvation . . . ; He was acquainted with the situation of all nations and with their destiny; He ordered all things according to the council of His own will; He knows the situation of both the living and the dead, and has made ample provision for their redemption, according to their several circumstances, and the laws of the kingdom of God, whether in this world, or in the world to come."[27]

We all have access to light for the journey home, and we can all be directed by the spirit of revelation proceeding from the Almighty and obtain the intelligence we need to find our way safely back. The Holy Ghost can show us "all things what [we] should do" (2 Nephi 32:5). We are not alone. As President Lorenzo Snow declared, it is the "grand privilege of every Latter-day Saint . . . to have the manifestations of the spirit every day of our lives. . . . This is a grand means that the Lord has provided for us, that we may know the light, and not be groveling continually in the dark."[28] The challenge is not in getting the Lord to speak to us but in learning to listen to what the Spirit has to say.

Notes

1. Young, *Millennial Star* 25 (1875): 597–98, as cited in Marion G. Romney, Conference Report, April 1944, 140–41.
2. Woodruff, *Deseret Weekly* 53 (7 November 1896): 643.
3. Smith, *Teachings*, 298.
4. Smith, *Teachings*, 299.
5. Smith, *Teachings*, 205.
6. Smith, *Teachings*, 205.
7. Smith, *Teachings*, 350.
8. McKay, *True to the Faith*, 244.
9. McKay, *Gospel Ideals*, 202.
10. Maxwell, *Ensign*, May 1985, 72.
11. Smith, *Teachings*, 324.
12. Ashton, *Ensign*, November 1992, 22.
13. Smith, *History of the Church*, 3:94.
14. Smith, *Teachings*, 70.
15. Smith, *Teachings*, 256.
16. Cannon, 1 March 1891, as cited in Stuy, *Collected Discourses*, 2:185.
17. Eyring, Conference Report, October 1996, 40.
18. Benson, Conference Report, April 1965, 121.

19. Young, Secretary's Journal, 28 January 1857, as cited in Maxwell, *Ensign*, November 1982, 67.
20. Maxwell, *Ensign*, November 1982, 67.
21. Benson, *Teachings*, 361.
22. McConkie, *Mortal Messiah*, 2:122.
23. Bateman, "Brigham Young University in the New Millennium."
24. Smith,*Teachings*, 304.
25. Young, *Journal of Discourses*, 7:275.
26. Cannon, 1 March 1891, as cited in Stuy, *Collected Discourses*, 2:185.
27. Smith, *Teachings*, 220.
28. Snow, Conference Report, April 1899, 52.

CHAPTER 4

"I Have Learned *for* Myself"

Is the Lord as interested in answering our prayers today as he was in the times of Adam and Eve, Daniel, or any of the ancient prophets? The Prophet Joseph pondered this same question as he prepared himself to go before God in secret prayer. Although he was only fourteen years of age, he felt deeply and contemplated seriously. He was drawn to James 1:5 and read it over and over: "If any of you lack wisdom, let him ask of God, that giveth to all men liberally, and upbraideth not; and it shall be given him." He said, "At length I came to the conclusion that I must either remain in darkness and confusion, or else I must do as James directs, that is, ask of God. I . . . came to the determination to 'ask of God,' concluding that if he gave wisdom to them that lacked wisdom, and would give liberally, and not upbraid, I might venture" (Joseph Smith–History 1:13).

The result of Joseph's faith and efforts was the First Vision. He declared, "I have learned for myself" (Joseph Smith–History 1:20). But what about us? We are not called to be prophets, as was Joseph Smith. We need revelation, but none of us would have the temerity to suggest we're seeking the kind of revelation that Joseph experienced, the kind that would change the world. But we do need revelation to change our personal worlds. Can we get help from God to find peace and serenity for our own lives? Absolutely. That is precisely the purpose of revelation: "For my Spirit is sent forth into the world to enlighten the humble and contrite" (D&C 136:33).

The Desire to Know

When Nephi desired to see and know what his father had learned by revelation, he humbly sought God and received all that he asked—and more:

"And it came to pass after I, Nephi, having heard all the words of my father, concerning the things which he saw in a vision, and also the things which he spake by the power of the Holy Ghost, which power he received by faith on the Son of God—and the Son of God was the Messiah who should come—I, Nephi, was desirous also that I might see, and hear, and know of these things, by the power of the Holy Ghost, which is the gift of God unto all those who diligently seek him" (1 Nephi 10:17).

Nephi spoke of three things that brought him the revelation he sought: he *desired* God's help, he *believed* (or *had faith*) that God could make things known to him, and he spent time in *prayer and pondering* (1 Nephi 11:1). The result? He was caught away in the Spirit of the Lord and shown all things he desired to know, plus much more (1 Nephi 11–14).

The Prophet Joseph said that "all the minds and spirits that God ever sent into the world are susceptible of enlargement."[1] That means every soul is able to receive enlightenment and revelation. But even seasoned members of the Church may not know when they are receiving a witness of the Spirit. Perhaps we are so surrounded by the influence of the Spirit that we fail to recognize it (3 Nephi 9:20) or perhaps we just take it for granted, or perhaps we are looking for something so dramatic that we do not understand the feelings of serenity, peace, and well-being associated with the Spirit.

The Prophet Joseph described how anxious God is to bless us: "Our heavenly Father is more liberal in His views, and boundless in His mercies and blessings, than we are ready to believe or receive. . . . He will be inquired of by His children. He says, 'Ask and ye shall receive, seek and ye shall find;' . . . no good thing will I withhold from them who walk uprightly before me, and do my will in all things—who will listen to my voice and to the voice of my servant whom I have sent; for I delight in those who seek diligently to know my precepts, and abide the law of my kingdom; for all things shall be made known unto them in mine own due time, and in the end they shall have joy."[2]

The Lord rewards us according to the desire of our hearts (D&C 137:9). When Martin Harris desired to see the Book of Mormon plates, the Lord chastised him for his pride but then promised him the desire of his heart: "Behold, I say unto him, he exalts himself and does not humble himself sufficiently before me; but if he will bow down before me, and humble himself in mighty prayer and faith, in the sincerity of his heart, then will I grant unto him a view of the things which he desires to see" (D&C 5:24). The Prophet Joseph taught us to "remember [that] God sees the secret springs of human action, and knows the hearts of all living. . . . God has respect to the feelings of His Saints."[3]

But the Prophet also warned that revelation is precious and sacred. It is not to be taken for granted. It comes in response to much humility and prayer: "We never inquire at the hand of God for special revelation only in case of their being no previous revelation to suit the case. . . . It is a great thing to inquire at the hands of God, or to come into His presence; and we feel fearful to approach Him on subjects that are of little or no consequence, to satisfy the queries of individuals, especially about things the knowledge of which men ought to obtain in all sincerity, before God, for themselves, in humility by the prayer of faith."[4]

Revelations do come, and the Lord prompts us with impressions and feelings far more than we realize or give him credit for: "Behold, I have manifested unto you, by my Spirit in many instances" (D&C 18:2; see also Jarom 1:4). Nephi and Lehi, the sons of Helaman, had "many revelations daily" (Helaman 11:23) and recognized them. Perhaps we do not always recognize the testimony of the Spirit because it occurs so regularly. "For many," Elder Loren C. Dunn reminds us, "the challenge lies not in receiving promptings from the Spirit, but in following them."[5]

Each of us has access to the same scriptures and is entitled to the same guidance of the Holy Spirit. But each must pay the price set by God in order to gain personal revelation. Here are some ways that we can learn for ourselves the influence of the Spirit in our lives.

Humility, Key to Revelation

Humility before God, especially in times of trouble, is one of the keys that unlocks revelation from heaven. The pioneers began their trek into the wilderness with this counsel from God: "Let him that is ignorant learn wisdom by humbling himself and calling upon the Lord his God, that his eyes may be opened that he may see, and his ears opened that he may hear" (D&C 136:32). All of us are "ignorant" and in need of wisdom beyond our own. Hence Alma's reassuring counsel: "I wish from the inmost part of my heart . . . that ye would humble yourselves before the Lord, and call on his holy name, and watch and pray continually, that ye may not be tempted above that which ye can bear, and thus be led by the Holy Spirit" (Alma 13:27–28).

One of the most often-repeated commandments in the scriptures is "ask and you shall receive." God delights in giving his children revelation. When it was reported to Moses that others were receiving revelation (besides the seventy who had been called), he was asked to forbid them, to prevent it. Instead, he responded, "Enviest thou for my sake? would God that all the Lord's people were prophets, and that the Lord would put his spirit upon them!" (Numbers 11:29).

Through the Prophet Joseph the Lord has promised us: "If thou shalt ask, thou shalt receive revelation upon revelation, knowledge upon knowledge, that thou mayest know the mysteries and peaceable things—that which bringeth joy, that which bringeth life eternal" (D&C 42:61). God is eager to reveal whatever we need to return to his presence.

We can have faith that humble petitions to him are answered. Elder Orson F. Whitney shared an experience showing how perfectly willing God is to answer our immediate solicitations for help: "I found myself in an overworked, run-down condition, manifesting a decided lack of physical and mental vigor. . . . One morning I was endeavoring to write the usual editorial [for the *Millennial Star*], but could make no headway, and wore out the whole day in a vain attempt to produce something worth reading. At last I threw down my pen and burst into tears of vexation.

"Just then the Good Spirit whispered: 'Why don't you pray?'

"As if a voice had addressed me audibly, I answered, 'I do pray.' I was praying five times a day—secret prayers, morning, noon and night; and vocal prayers, with the rest of the household, at breakfast and dinner time. 'I do pray—why can't I get some help,' I asked, almost petulantly, for I was heartsick and half-discouraged.

"'Pray now,' said the Spirit, 'and ask for what you want.'

"I saw the point. It was a special, not a general, prayer that was needed. I knelt and sobbed out a few simple words. I did not pray for the return of the Ten Tribes nor for the building of the New Jerusalem. I asked the Lord in the name of Jesus Christ to help me write that article. I then arose, seated myself, and began to write. My mind was now perfectly clear, and my pen fairly flew over the paper. All I needed came as fast as I could set it down—every thought, every word in place. In a short time the article was completed to my entire satisfaction."[6]

Yielding to the Enticings of the Spirit

Joseph Smith was taught that while we are experiencing mortality, we must learn to yield to the whisperings of the Lord's Spirit. The fallen condition we find ourselves in has had an effect on everything, including our spirituality. We are eternal, spiritual beings in a mortal moment. We once dwelt in God's presence and enjoyed his Spirit and blessings abundantly. We now find ourselves separated from him, but we can have his Spirit and his blessings here if we are humble and obedient: "For the natural man is an enemy to God, and has been from the fall of Adam, and will be, forever and ever, unless he yields to the enticings of the Holy Spirit, and putteth off the natural man and becometh a saint through the atonement of Christ the Lord, and becometh as a child, submissive, meek, humble, patient, full of love, willing to submit to all things which the Lord seeth fit to inflict upon him, even as a child doth submit to his father" (Mosiah 3:19). Only by "yielding" and "submitting" to spiritual enticings can we become like the Savior. He set the perfect example of yielding his will to the Father and invites us to follow him (2 Nephi 31:5–9; 3 Nephi 27:27).

God's Spirit is not one of force or coercion. He invites and entices but never compels. We are free to choose for ourselves and are thus enabled to grow. The Prophet Joseph learned this truth early in his calling. On one occasion he was asked how he governed his people. He replied: "I teach the people correct principles and they govern themselves."[7] He also said, "In relation to the power over the minds of mankind which I hold, I would say, It is in consequence of the power of truth in the doctrines which I have been an instrument in the hands of God of presenting unto them, and not because of any compulsion on my part."[8] Today we sing a hymn (published in the first Latter-day Saint hymnbook) that summarizes this same truth:

Know this, that ev'ry soul is free
To choose his life and what he'll be;
For this eternal truth is giv'n:
That God will force no man to heav'n.
He'll call, persuade, direct aright,
And bless with wisdom, love, and light,
In nameless ways be good and kind,
But never force the human mind.[9]

Developing Spiritual Capacity

When asked why we are sometimes left alone to make choices, President Brigham Young answered that man is destined to be a God and has to act as an independent being "to practice . . . using his own resources . . . to be righteous in the dark . . . to be a friend of God."[10] He encouraged the Saints to develop self-reliance that is subject to the Spirit:

"Now those men, or those women, who know no more about the power of God, and the influences of the Holy Spirit, than to be led entirely by another person, suspending their own understanding, and pinning their faith upon another's sleeve, will never be capable of entering into the celestial glory, to be crowned as they anticipate; they will never be capable of becoming Gods. They cannot rule themselves, to say nothing of ruling others, but they must be dictated to in every trifle, like a child. They cannot control themselves in the least, but James, Peter, or somebody else must control them. They never can become Gods, nor be crowned as rulers with glory, immortality, and eternal lives. They never can hold sceptres of glory, majesty, and power in the celestial kingdom. Who will? Those who are valiant and inspired with the true independence of heaven, who will go forth boldly in the service of their God, leaving others to do as they please. . . . Will this apply to any of you? Your own hearts can answer."[11]

We bring with us the capacity to grow in light and truth. The Prophet Joseph revealed that in our premortal life we achieved varying levels of spiritual understanding and commitment by the exercise of our agency (Abraham 3:22–28; Alma 13:1–9). We bring with us our premortal personalities. So, although we are all born into mortality equally innocent (D&C 93:38–39), we do not come equally prepared to remain innocent because we bring with us the "nature" we developed before we were born. Elder Bruce R. McConkie said, "We know we were schooled and trained and taught in the most perfect educational system ever devised, and that by obedience to his eternal laws we developed infinite varieties and degrees of talents. . . . When we come into mortality, we bring the talents, capacities, and abilities acquired by obedience to law in our prior existence."[12]

Elder McConkie also said that of all the talents that could be developed in the premortal life, spirituality was the greatest: "Men are born into mortality with the talents and abilities acquired by obedience to law in their first estate. Above all talents—greater than any other capacities, chief among all endowments—stands the talent for spirituality. Those so endowed find it easy to believe the truth in this life."[13]

All have access to the light of Christ. Those who hearken to that light continue in God's Spirit and are eventually brought to the fulness of the gospel (Moroni 7:14–19; D&C 88:5–13; 84:45–48; 93:31–32). As we exercise our agency throughout mortality by responding to or resisting heavenly promptings, our "natures" are continually developing. If we respond sufficiently to the promptings and accept the gospel, the Holy Ghost can change us "from [our] carnal and fallen state, to a state of righteousness, being redeemed of God, becoming his sons and daughters . . . [and] new creatures" (Mosiah 27:25–26). If we do not respond to such an opportunity, we remain as a "natural man," described as "an enemy to God" (Mosiah 3:19), "without God in the world" (Alma 41:1), or "carnal, sensual, and devilish" (Alma 42:10). At death we take with us into the spirit world whatever nature we have developed to that time. There the gospel will be taught to "all the spirits of men" (D&C 138:30). The level of light and truth people will accept in the spirit world will likely depend upon the same factors that influenced our choices here on earth and in the premortal world—our natures, inclinations, agency, and the desires of our heart to follow the Spirit.

Once we have experienced premortality, earth life, and the postearthly spirit world, we will have had adequate opportunity to learn and understand the gospel of Jesus Christ and to demonstrate what we really are, what measure of light and truth we really desire, what glory we are willing and able to abide. And God has prepared kingdoms of varying glories and degrees to accommodate everyone's choice. Becoming a son or daughter of God is different from being a spirit child of Heavenly Father. The words "sons of God" (1 John 3:1–2) refer to those who accept Christ and his gospel, take upon themselves the name of Christ through baptism, honor his name through faith and righteousness, and become sanctified through the Spirit (D&C 25:1; 45:8).

We really are free to choose our lives and what we will become. Each day there can be a new beginning. It is a choice. It is our choice. "Therefore, cheer up your hearts, and remember that ye are free to act for yourselves—to choose the way of everlasting death or the way of eternal life" (2 Nephi 10:23; 2:27). Little wonder, with so much riding on how well we exercise our agency, that Satan targets all of his efforts to get us to make wrong choices. It really does matter! Joseph Smith observed, "The nearer a person approaches the Lord, a greater power [will] be manifest by the Devil to prevent the accomplishment of the purposes of God."[14] But we have no need to fear. The Lord is always there to help. Satan has never had total power or control. We should never take counsel from fear but only from our faith in the Savior: "Despise not, and wonder not, but hearken unto the words of the Lord, and ask the Father in the name of Jesus for what things soever ye shall stand in need. Doubt not, but be believing" (Mormon 9:27). Like Alma's people, we should hush our fears and cry unto the Lord (Mosiah 23:28).

President Woodruff said that we need to labor to get the Lord's Spirit because "we are surrounded by these evil spirits that are at war against God and against everything looking to the building up of the kingdom of God; and we need this Holy Spirit to enable us to overcome these influences."[15] Those who are faithful (who have faith) will "overcome all things, and be lifted up [into the celestial kingdom] at the last day" (D&C 75:22; 76:60).

The Prophet Joseph Smith was told, "They who are of a celestial spirit shall receive" a celestial body in the resurrection (D&C 88:28). Living the gospel, developing a righteous heart, celestially educating the desires of our heart, and learning to live the law of the celestial kingdom to the best of our ability in mortality will help us to live in celestial glory in the next life (D&C 88:21–24).

Faith Comes by Hearing the Word

In the *Lectures on Faith*, the Prophet Joseph indicated that hearing the testimony of others motivates people to want to know for ourselves: "We have seen that it was human testimony, and human testimony only, that excited this inquiry, in the first instance, in their minds. . . . It was the credence they gave to the testimony of their fathers, this testimony having aroused their minds to inquire after the knowledge of God; the inquiry frequently terminated, indeed always terminated when rightly pursued, in the most glorious discoveries and eternal certainty."[16]

We often live beneath our privileges. President Brigham Young was concerned that the Saints did not seek more often to learn from the light of revelation: "Herein is where mankind fail, lacking that which we might have in our possession, viz.—the light of the revelations of Jesus Christ, the light of the Holy Spirit, the light of heaven. This is the privilege of the Latter-day Saints, but they do not enjoy it as much as they might."[17]

But just hearing the testimony of others is not enough. Only obedience, to the best of our ability, secures the blessings. The Prophet Joseph said, "Will the mere admission that this is the will of heaven ever benefit us if we do not comply with all its teachings? Do we not offer violence to the Supreme Intelligence of heaven, when we admit the truth of its teachings, and do not obey them? Do we not descend below our own knowledge, and the better wisdom which heaven has endowed us with, by such a course of conduct? For these reasons, if we have direct revelations given us from heaven, surely those revelations were never given to be trifled with, without the trifler's incurring displeasure and vengence upon his own head."[18]

God has never given any revelation through his prophets to harm us. All his revelations are intended to bless us and to help us know what we need to do to return to his presence. The Prophet Joseph said, "Everything that God gives us is lawful and right; and it is proper that we should enjoy His gifts and blessings whenever and wherever He is disposed to bestow. . . . As God has designed our happiness—and the happiness of all His creatures, he never has—He never will institute an ordinance or give a commandment to His people that is not calculated in its nature to promote that happiness which He has designed, and which will not end in the greatest amount of good and glory to those who become the recipients of his law and ordinances."[19]

No Longer Standing on Borrowed Light

President Heber C. Kimball once prophesied that each person would need to draw close to the light of revelation to pass the tests of mortality. Speaking to the Saints who had settled in the Rocky Mountains twenty years before, President Kimball declared: "We think we are secure here in the chambers of the everlasting hills, where we can close those few doors of the canyons against mobs and persecutors, the wicked and the vile who have always beset us with violence and robbery; but I want to say to you, my brethren, the time is coming when we will be mixed up in these now peaceful valleys to that extent that it will be difficult to tell the face of a Saint from the face of an enemy to the people of God. Then, brethren, look out for the great sieve, for there will be a great sifting time, and many will fall, for I say unto you, there is a test, a TEST, a TEST, coming, and who will be able to stand? . . .

"You imagine that you would have stood by [the Prophet Joseph Smith] when persecution raged, and he was assailed by foes within and without. You would have defended him, and been true to him in the midst of every trial. You think you would have been delighted to have shown your integrity in the days of mobs and traitors.

"Let me say to you, that many of you will see the time when you will have all the trouble, trial and persecution that you can stand, and plenty of opportunities to show that you are true to God and His work. This Church has before it many close places through which it will have to pass before the work of God is crowned with victory. To meet the difficulties that are coming, it will be necessary for you to have a knowledge of the truth of this work for yourselves; the difficulties will be of such a character that the man or woman who does not possess this personal knowledge or witness will fall. If you have not got the testimony, live right, and call upon the Lord and cease not until you obtain it. If you do not you will not stand. . . .

"Remember these sayings, for many of you will live to see them fulfilled. The time will come when no man nor woman will be able to endure on borrowed light. Each will have to be guided by the light within himself. If you do not have it, how can you stand?"[20]

Elder J. Golden Kimball later repeated his father's warning, adding, "If the Latter-day Saints do not know that Jesus is the Christ, and that this is His Church, I tell you, in the name of the Lord, you will not stand, you will be among the number that will fall."[21]

Also quoting President Heber C. Kimball's prophecy, President Harold B. Lee said, "This is the time of which President Kimball spoke, when each will have to stand on his own feet, and no man will be able to exist and stand on borrowed light. Each, for himself, must have an unshakeable testimony of the divinity of this work if he is to stand in this day!"[22]

Strength to Withstand Trials

If the Prophet Joseph Smith had not had his own witness from heaven, he could never have withstood the tests and trials he was subjected to. Brigham Young once said, "If a thousand hounds were on this Temple Block [Temple Square], let loose on one rabbit, it would not be a bad illustration of the situation at times of the Prophet Joseph. He was hunted unremittingly."[23]

The Prophet wrote of the depth of his commitment and his willingness to stand by the witness he had received: "I had actually seen a light, and in the midst of that light I saw two Personages, and they did in reality speak to me; and though I was hated and persecuted for saying that I had seen a vision, yet it was true; and while they were persecuting me, reviling me, and speaking all manner of evil against me falsely for so saying, I was led to say in my heart: Why persecute me for telling the truth? I have actually seen a vision; and who am I that I can withstand God, or why does the world think to make me deny what I have actually seen? For I had seen a vision; I knew it, and I knew that God knew it, and I could not deny it, neither dared I do it; at least I knew that by so doing I would offend God, and come under condemnation" (Joseph Smith–History 1:24–25).

None of us can stand without God's help, and none of us will ever be able to stand in his presence without the help of the Spirit to lead and guide us through life. True conversion, enduring conversion, comes only from the witness of the Spirit. It is available to all, and, as President Ezra Taft Benson noted, it really does make a difference: "Social, ethical, cultural, or educational converts will not survive under the heat of the day unless their taproots go down to the fulness of the gospel."[24] As did the Prophet Joseph Smith, we must all learn for ourselves that the Restoration is real, that God has spoken again to men on the earth, and that he will speak to us and bless us in time of need—else how can we stand?

In the early years of the Restoration, Hiram Page, one of the eight witnesses to the Book of Mormon, obtained a stone through which he received several so-called revelations that led other Church members away from the truth. President Harold B. Lee summarized the lessons learned from that and similar experiences:

"From the days of Hiram Page, at different periods there have been manifestations from delusive spirits to members of the Church. . . .

"When visions, dreams, tongues, prophecy, impressions or any extraordinary gift or inspiration conveys something out of harmony with the accepted revelations of the Church or contrary to the decisions of its constituted authorities, Latter-day Saints may know that it is not of God, no matter how plausible it may appear. Also, they should understand that directions for the guidance of the Church will come, by revelation, through the head. All faithful members are entitled to the inspiration of the Holy Spirit for themselves, their families, and for those over whom they are appointed and ordained to preside. But anything at discord with that which comes from God through the head of the Church is not to be received as authoritative or reliable."[25]

We need to learn for ourselves so we can stand on the strength of our own testimony. Humility, yielding to the enticings of the Spirit, developing spiritual capacity, and increasing faith by receiving the word of the Lord in our minds and hearts will help us be guided by the light within.

Notes

1. Smith, *Teachings*, 354.
2. Smith, *Teachings*, 257.
3. Smith, *Teachings*, 19.
4. Smith, *Teachings*, 22.
5. Dunn, "Unity in the Faith," 62.
6. Whitney, *Through Memory's Halls*, 215.
7. Taylor, *Journal of Discourses*, 10:57–58.
8. Smith, *History of the Church*, 6:273.

9. "Know This, That Every Soul Is Free," *Hymns*, no. 240.
10. President's Office Journal, 28 January 1857, Brigham Young Papers, LDS Church Archives, Salt Lake City, as cited in Maxwell, *Even As I Am*, 46.
11. Young, *Journal of Discourses*, 1:312.
12. McConkie, *Ensign*, May 1974, 73.
13. McConkie, *Millennial Messiah*, 234.
14. Whitney, *Heber C. Kimball Journal*, 18, as cited in *Woman's Exponent* 9 (1880): 18.
15. Woodruff, *Deseret Weekly* (7 November 1896): 643, as cited in Stuy, *Collected Discourses*, vol. 5.
16. Smith, *Lectures on Faith*, 24.
17. Young, *Journal of Discourses*, 2:300.
18. Smith, *History of the Church*, 2:11.
19. Smith, *Teachings*, 256–57.
20. Heber C. Kimball, as cited in J. Golden Kimball, Conference Report, April 1906, 76.
21. J. Golden Kimball, Conference Report, April 1906, 77.
22. Lee, *Teachings of Harold B. Lee*, 144.
23. Young, *Discourses of Brigham Young*, 464.
24. Benson, *Witness and a Warning*, 6.
25. Lee, *Improvement Era*, June 1970, 63–64.

CHAPTER 5

Recognizing the Voice of the Spirit

The Lord can speak to us in many different ways, but most often he uses what we refer to as a still small voice (D&C 1:4, 14; 88:89–90). "We do not have the words (even the scriptures do not have words)," Elder Boyd K. Packer observed, "which perfectly describe the Spirit. The scriptures generally use the word *voice*, which does not exactly fit. These delicate, refined spiritual communications are not seen with our eyes, nor heard with our ears. And even though it is described as a voice, it is a voice that one feels, more than one hears."[1]

When the Spirit speaks to our souls, it doesn't shout with a "voice of thunder" or make "a great tumultuous noise" but uses "a still voice of perfect mildness, as if it had been a whisper" (Helaman 5:30). It is more powerful than thunder. It is the kind of voice that "whispereth through and pierceth all things" (D&C 85:6). Yet it is a "pleasant voice" (Helaman 5:46).

The promptings of the Spirit are often not dramatic. In fact, President Spencer W. Kimball taught that if we look for the intensely dramatic we could overlook many revelations: "In our day, as in times past, many people expect that if there be revelation it will come with awe-inspiring, earthshaking display. For many it is hard to accept as revelation those numerous ones in Moses' time, in Joseph's time, and in our own year—those revelations which come to prophets as deep, unassailable impressions settling down on the prophet's mind and heart as dew from heaven or as the dawn dissipates the darkness of night.

Expecting the spectacular, one may not be fully alerted to the constant flow of revealed communication."[2]

The Prophet Joseph Smith cautioned that "the Lord cannot always be known by the thunder of His voice, by the display of His glory or by the manifestation of His power, and those that are the most anxious to see these things, are the least prepared to meet them."[3]

Elder Boyd K. Packer has similarly testified: "I have learned that strong, impressive spiritual experiences do not come to us very frequently. And when they do, they are generally for our own edification, instruction, or correction."[4]

Feeling the Spirit

The whisperings of the Spirit resonate within our heart and pierce us "even to the very soul" (Helaman 5:30). Joseph Smith said that when the Holy Ghost speaks to us, his communication goes to our spirits "precisely as though we had no bodies at all."[5]

Revelation is a spiritual communication to the mind or heart. The promptings of the Holy Spirit are like food for the soul. They come as thoughts, feelings, impressions, or promptings. By heeding the sudden ideas that come into the mind or the feelings that inspire us to action, we can receive revelation in the hour of our need. President Ezra Taft Benson said: "We hear the words of the Lord most often by a feeling. If we are humble and sensitive, the Lord will prompt us through our feelings. . . . Being in tune with the Spirit of the Lord is the greatest need of all of us."[6]

True spiritual feelings are so refined that some fail to recognize them. Nephi said to his brothers, "Ye have heard [God's] voice from time to time; and he hath spoken unto you in a still small voice, but ye were past feeling, that ye could not feel his words" (1 Nephi 17:45). The words spoken by the Spirit are words that have to be *felt* rather than heard, and the *ear* by which we hear the Spirit of the Lord is the *heart* (3 Nephi 11:3–6).

There are times, however, when the voice of the Spirit is so strong within us that it almost seems as if we are being instructed by an audible voice. Such an event happened to an attorney who was asked to represent the Prophet Joseph Smith. In the fall of 1830, the Prophet was arrested in Colesville, New York, on a trumped-up charge. John Reid was asked to serve as Joseph's attorney. Mr. Reid described the experience he had hearing the voice of the Spirit: "I was so busy at that time, when Mr. Smith sent for me, that it was almost impossible for me to attend the case, and never having seen Mr. Smith, I determined to decline going. But soon after coming to this conclusion, I thought I heard someone say to me, 'You *must* go, and deliver the Lord's Anointed!' Supposing it was the man who came after me, I replied, 'The Lord's Anointed? What do you mean by the Lord's Anointed?' He was surprised at being accosted in this manner, and replied, 'What do you mean, sir? I said nothing about the Lord's Anointed.' I was convinced that he told the truth, for these few words filled my mind with peculiar feelings, such as I had never before experienced; and I immediately hastened to the place of trial. Whilst I was engaged in the case, these emotions increased, and when I came to speak upon it, I was inspired with an eloquence which was altogether new to me, and which was overpowering and irresistible. I succeeded, as I expected, in obtaining the prisoner's discharge."[7]

Many times members of the Church feel the influence of the Holy Ghost but may not be aware that the feelings they are experiencing are from the Spirit. President Boyd K. Packer has said, "Too many of us are like those whom the Lord said '[came] with a broken heart and a contrite spirit, . . . [and] at the time of their conversion, were baptized with fire and with the Holy Ghost, *and they knew it not*.' (3 Nephi 9:20; emphasis added.) Imagine that: 'And they knew it not.' It is not unusual for one to have received the gift and not really know it."[8]

What does it feel like when the Spirit speaks to us? Let us consider several examples.

Peace and Joy

Impressions from the Spirit are usually associated with deep feelings of peace, abiding feelings of serenity, or a pervasive feeling of well-being. "Verily, verily, I say unto you," the Lord told Joseph Smith, "I will impart unto you of my Spirit, which shall enlighten . . . your soul with joy; and then shall ye know, or by this shall you know, all things whatsoever you desire of me, which are pertaining unto things of righteousness, in faith believing in me that you shall receive" (D&C 11:13–14). These impressions are often accompanied by a warmth, an assurance, or a confirmation of specific direction. "You will find," Elder Loren C. Dunn of the Seventy taught, "that such impressions will be in harmony with the scriptures, with the Church, and usually with good common sense."[9]

To Oliver Cowdery, who was asking whether or not he should assist Joseph Smith, the Lord declared, "If you desire a further witness, cast your mind upon the night that you cried unto me in your heart, that you might know concerning the truth of these things. Did I not speak peace to your mind concerning the matter? What greater witness can you have than from God?" (D&C 6:22–23).

Thoughts and Feelings

The Spirit can communicate with us in unlimited ways, but the most common way is through thoughts and feelings. Joseph had learned while translating the Book of Mormon to pay close attention to the thoughts and feelings that came to him. The Savior had counseled him, "Yea, behold, I will tell you in your mind and in your heart, by the Holy Ghost, which shall come upon you and which shall dwell in your heart. Now, behold, this is the spirit of revelation" (D&C 8:2–3).

Years later, while writing a letter of instruction to the Saints, Joseph observed: "As I stated to you in my letter before I left my place, that I would write to you from time to time and give you information in relation to many subjects, I now resume the subject of the baptism for the dead, as that subject seems to occupy my mind, and press itself upon my feelings the strongest" (D&C 128:1).

Thoughts that occupy our minds or press themselves upon our

feelings most strongly may be the most common way the Spirit speaks to us. Learning to listen to Spirit-prompted feelings that press themselves upon us (feelings of urgency or impressions to do or to refrain from doing something) and learning to pay attention to the thoughts that come suddenly to our minds are ways of learning to hear the voice of the Spirit. The Prophet Joseph said, "A person may profit by noticing the first intimation of the spirit of revelation; for instance, when you feel pure intelligence flowing into you, it may give you sudden strokes of ideas, so that by noticing it, you may find it fulfilled the same day or soon; (i.e.) those things that were presented unto your minds by the Spirit of God, will come to pass; and thus by learning the Spirit of God and understanding it, you may grow into the principle of revelation, until you become perfect in Christ Jesus."[10]

Revelation comes often as a "sudden stroke of intelligence," an idea to our mind or a feeling in our heart: "Behold, thou knowest that thou hast inquired of me and I did enlighten thy mind; and now I tell thee these things that thou mayest know that thou hast been enlightened by the Spirit of truth" (D&C 6:15).

In the scriptures the prophets wrote that—more often than visions, more often than dreams, and more often than the appearance of angels—"the voice of the Lord came into my mind" (Enos 1:10) or the "voice of the Lord came unto me" (1 Nephi 17:7; Mormon 3:14). For example, when Moses led the children of Israel out of Egypt towards the promised land, they were pursued by the Egyptian army and trapped on the shores of the Red Sea. Only the pillar of fire—a physical pillar of light but a spiritual reminder that they were guided and protected by the Spirit—held the enemy army at bay (Exodus 14). It would have been powerfully convincing if God's voice had thundered from the heavens "PART THE SEA!" or if an angel had appeared to deliver the message. But the still, small voice of the Spirit reminded Moses of the promise he had been given many years before: "Blessed art thou, Moses, for I, the Almighty, have chosen thee, and thou shalt be made stronger than many waters; for they shall obey thy command as if thou wert God" (Moses 1:25). The spirit of revelation came into Moses' mind and heart at the moment he needed it: "Behold, I will tell you in your mind and in your heart, by the Holy Ghost. . . . Now, behold, this is the spirit of revelation; behold, this is the spirit by which Moses brought the children of Israel through the Red Sea on dry ground" (D&C 8:2–3).

It must have taken great courage to stand before the frightened children of Israel and act on a prompting that only he received. But Moses had that courage. He was "very meek, above all the men which were upon the face of the earth" (Numbers 12:3). Meekness is the courage and internal strength to do as the Lord commands, regardless of the consequences. With great confidence and trust in God, Moses said to the people, "Fear ye not, stand still, and see the salvation of the Lord, which he will shew to you [Hebrew, 'accomplish for you'] to day: for the Egyptians whom ye have seen to day, ye shall see them again no more" (Exodus 14:13).

Nephi demonstrated this moral courage when he said to his brothers, who wanted to return home without fulfilling the Lord's command to obtain the brass plates from Laban, "I was led by the Spirit, not knowing beforehand the things which I should do. Nevertheless," he declared, "I went forth" (1 Nephi 4:6–7).

Mary also exhibited this same courage and faith when she responded to the angel Gabriel's announcement that she would be the mother of the Messiah: "Be it unto me according to thy word" (Luke 1:38).

Spirit-borne thoughts or impressions that come into our minds or hearts are revelation from the Lord. We might rationalize them away or allow our fears to convince us that the promptings are from our own wishes or hunches, but the impressions of the Spirit are real and are sent to help us in times of need: "Therefore, verily I say unto you . . . speak the thoughts that I shall put into your hearts, and you shall not be confounded before men; for it shall be given you in the very hour, yea, in the very moment, what ye shall say" (D&C 100:5–6).

The more closely in tune we are with the Spirit, the stronger the impressions become. While marching with Zion's Camp, the Prophet Joseph had an impression about a particular area through which they were traveling. He said, "We came into a piece of thick woods of recent growth, where I told [the men I was with] that I felt much depressed in spirit and lonesome, and that there had been a great deal of bloodshed in that place, remarking that whenever a man of God is in a place where many have been killed, he will feel lonesome and unpleasant, and his spirits will sink. In about forty rods from where I made this observation we came through the woods, and saw a large farm, and there near the road on our left, was a mound sixty feet high, containing human bones."[11]

Thoughts and impressions that occupy our attention or feelings, or dwell in our heart, may be from the still small voice of the Spirit. The danger of living in a society that moves at such a fast pace is that we may become too preoccupied to feel the spirit of revelation and to take the time to confirm that what we are feeling is indeed from the Spirit. "The things of God are of deep import," the Prophet Joseph said, "and time, and experience, and careful and ponderous and solemn thoughts can only find them out."[12]

The Lord often speaks to us through feelings and has promised that he will confirm our right decisions: "Therefore, you shall feel that it is right" (D&C 9:8). We sometimes refer to this confirmation as a "burning in the bosom." Elder Boyd K. Packer has said that "this burning in the bosom is not purely a physical sensation. It is more like a warm light shining within your being."[13] Elder Packer has also cautioned, "The Spirit does not get our attention by shouting or shaking us with a heavy hand. Rather it whispers. It caresses so gently that if we are preoccupied we may not feel it at all. . . .

"Occasionally it will press just firmly enough for us to pay heed. But most of the time, if we do not heed the gentle feeling, the Spirit will withdraw and wait until we come seeking and listening."[14] The "burning of the bosom" may be less dramatic—not less powerful but less dramatic—than we expect.

The Holy Ghost has power to reveal events to us through our thoughts and feelings even before those events happen. For instance, a person might be sitting in a room before a meeting is about to begin and suddenly feel the impression that he or she will be asked to offer the opening prayer; or a strong feeling may indicate to the heart that a new calling is coming; or a thought may enter the mind to do something that later proves to be a blessing. Such revelations from the Holy Ghost help us by giving us time to prepare for whatever is coming.

Judging by the Spirit

On occasion we may be asked to support what sounds like a good cause or a good idea. How can we judge? Moroni taught that there is a way for us to know when we've made a correct choice: "Wherefore, I show unto you the way to judge; for every thing which inviteth to do good, and to persuade to believe in Christ, is sent forth by the power and gift of Christ; wherefore ye may know with a perfect knowledge it is of God" (Moroni 7:16).

Note those two qualifications: it has to invite us to do good *and* to come unto Christ (1 John 4:1–3). If something sounds good or seems good but leads us away from Christ, his gospel, his teachings, or his prophets, we may know with perfect surety it is not from him: "But whatsoever thing persuadeth men to do evil, and believe not in Christ, and deny him, and serve not God, then ye may know with a perfect knowledge it is of the devil; for after this manner doth the devil work, for he persuadeth no man to do good, no, not one; neither do his angels, neither do they who subject themselves unto him" (Moroni 7:17).

How can we tell if something is misguiding us or is going to take us away from God? A simple way is to measure it against the teachings of the scriptures, the standard works. The scriptures are called standard works because they are the standards by which we can measure our works. "Measure it against the teachings of the prophets and apostles," Elder Vaughn J. Featherstone said. "If it moves you away from the Church or the doctrine, it is not of God."[15] For example, if the thought comes that we do not need to pray, we can measure it against the scriptures, which plainly teach that the Spirit would never propose such an idea (2 Nephi 32:8–9).

Using an incident from his own day, Joseph Smith shared an example illustrating how to measure supposed revelations against the revealed word of God: "There have also been ministering angels in the Church which were of Satan appearing as an angel of light. A sister in the state of New York had a vision, who said it was told her that if she would go to a certain place in the woods, an angel would appear to her. She went at the appointed time, and saw a glorious personage descending, arrayed in white . . . ; he commenced and told her to fear God, and said that her husband was called to do great things, but that he must not go more than one hundred miles from home, or he would not return; whereas God had called him to go to the ends of the earth, and he has since been more than one thousand miles from home, and is yet alive. Many true things were spoken by this personage, and many things that were false. How, it may be asked, was this known to be a bad angel? . . . by his contradicting a former revelation."[16]

Foreboding Feelings

The Holy Ghost can also give us feelings that we should not do something. These can take the form of foreboding feelings—not just nervousness but real hesitancy. Joseph Smith experienced such feelings on several occasions. In 1842, Mayor John C. Bennett of Nauvoo, who had committed grievous sins and lost the Spirit of the Lord, plotted against the Prophet's life. On one occasion, he invited Joseph Smith to join in a sham battle with groups of men from the Nauvoo Legion. The Spirit whispered to Joseph not to go. The Prophet wrote: "I was solicited by General Bennett to take command of the first cohort during the sham battle; this I declined. General Bennett next requested me to take my station in the rear of the cavalry, without my staff, during the engagement; but this was counteracted by Captain A. P. Rockwood, commander of my life guards, who kept close to my side, and I chose my own position. And if General Bennett's true feelings toward me are not made manifest to the world in a very short time, then it may be possible that the gentle breathings of that Spirit, which whispered to me on parade, that there was mischief concealed in that sham battle, were false; a short time will determine the point. Let John C. Bennett answer at the day of judgment, 'Why did you request me to command one of the cohorts, and also to take my position without my staff [body guards], during the sham battle, on the 7th of May, 1842, where my life might have been the forfeit, and no man have known who did the deed?'"[17]

Only heeding the promptings of the Holy Ghost saved Joseph from a tragedy. If we pay close attention to the promptings of the Spirit, the Holy Ghost can help us perceive, when necessary, the thoughts of others (Alma 18:16), the intentions in their hearts (Mosiah 13:5, 7, 11), dangerous trends in society (Alma 45:10), fears in the hearts of those we love (Alma 43:48), future events (Jacob 1:5), and troubling questions in the hearts of our children (Alma 40:1; 41:1; 42:1).

Truly one of the sweetest blessings in mortality is to cultivate a pondering mind and a tender heart in order to learn how to be guided by the Spirit of the Lord. Having the guidance of the Spirit "is a supernal gift. Indeed, it is a guide and a protection."[18]

Promise of Enlightenment

By the power of the Spirit, our eyes can be opened, and our understandings enlightened (D&C 76:12). When Joseph Smith and Sidney Rigdon were pondering the scriptures and working on the Joseph Smith Translation of the Bible, the Savior revealed a very special promise: "Thus saith the Lord—I, the Lord, am merciful and gracious unto those who fear me, and delight to honor those who serve me in righteousness and in truth unto the end.

"Great shall be their reward and eternal shall be their glory.

"And to them will I reveal all mysteries, yea, all the hidden mysteries of my kingdom from days of old, and for ages to come, will I make known unto them the good pleasure of my will concerning all things pertaining to my kingdom.

"Yea, even the wonders of eternity shall they know, and things to come will I show them, even the things of many generations.

"And their wisdom shall be great, and their understanding reach to heaven; and before them the wisdom of the wise shall perish, and the understanding of the prudent shall come to naught.

"For by my Spirit will I enlighten them, and by my power will I make known unto them the secrets of my will—yea, even those things which eye has not seen, nor ear heard, nor yet entered into the heart of man" (D&C 76:5–10).

When No Answer Comes

What do we do when no answer comes? Why does it seem as if some prayers are not answered? How do we proceed when we have no compelling feelings about what to do nor any compelling feelings about what to refrain from doing? Elder Boyd K. Packer counseled: "Sometimes you may struggle with a problem and not get an answer. What could be wrong? It may be that you are not doing anything wrong. It may be that you have not done the right things long enough. Remember, you cannot force spiritual things. Sometimes we are confused simply because we won't take no for an answer. . . . Put difficult questions in the back of your minds and go about your lives. Ponder and pray quietly and persistently about them. The answer may not come as a lightning bolt. It may come as a little inspiration here and a little there, 'line upon line, precept upon precept' (D&C 98:12). Some answers will come from reading the scriptures, some from hearing speakers. And, occasionally, when it is important, some will come by very direct and powerful inspiration. The promptings will be clear and unmistakable."[19]

It is important to remember, too, that we are here to learn and grow. Growth comes through participation, and God has designed our mortal probation so that our participation is maximized. Some decisions are left entirely up to us. To two missionaries departing for the mission field in 1832, the Lord said, "Go ye, go ye into the world and preach the gospel to every creature that cometh under the sound of your voice. . . . Wherefore, go ye and preach my gospel, whether to the north or to the south, to the east or to the west, it mattereth not, for ye cannot go amiss" (D&C 80:1, 3). It didn't matter which direction these two elders traveled in 1832 because there were many in every direction who had not yet had the opportunity to hear of the Restoration (D&C 123:12–14). The choice was theirs. When Joseph and some of the brethren were returning from Missouri to Kirtland, the

Lord indicated that it did not matter whether they traveled by water or by land (D&C 61:22) or whether they traveled together as a group or by twos (D&C 62:5). Some things don't matter. In those cases, any choice will be right.

President Brigham Young noted an important principle to remember when it seems like no revelation is forthcoming: we need to move forward in life and proceed to the best of our ability. "I will now refer you to the scripture, where it reads that we shall be judged according to the deeds done in the body," President Young said. "If I do not know the will of my Father, and what He requires of me in a certain transaction, if I ask Him to give me wisdom concerning any requirement in life, or in regard to my own course, or that of my friends, my family, my children, or those that I preside over, and get no answer from Him, and then do the very best that my judgment will teach me, He is bound to own and honor that transaction, and He will do so to all intents and purposes."[20] Elder Harold B. Lee once instructed Elder Boyd K. Packer, "You must learn to walk to the edge of the light, and perhaps a few steps into the darkness, and you will find that the light will appear and move ahead of you."[21] As we move forward, confirming witnesses come from the Lord. He has promised to guide and direct our paths as long as we are striving to stay close to his light. But the Lord's expectation is that we will go forward and do so to the best of our ability.

Elder John Groberg of the Seventy gave this wise advice to students during a devotional assembly:

"I have found that if that decision was wrong or was taking me down the wrong path—not necessarily an evil one, but one that was not right for me—without fail, the Lord has always let me know just this emphatically: 'That is wrong; do not go that way. That is not for you!'

"On the other hand, there may have been two or three ways that I could have gone, any one of which would have been right and would have been in the general area providing the experience and means whereby I could fulfill the mission that the Lord had in mind for me. Because he knows we need the growth, he generally does not point and say, 'Open that door and go twelve yards in that direction; then turn right and go two miles. . . .' But if it is wrong, he will let us know—we will feel it for sure. I am positive of that. So rather than saying, 'I will not move until I have this burning in my heart,' let us turn it around and say, 'I will move unless I feel it is wrong; and if it is wrong, then I will not do it.' By eliminating all of these wrong courses, very quickly you will find yourself going in the direction that you ought to be going, and then you can receive the assurance: 'Yes, I am going in the right direction.'"[22]

Thoughts that suddenly come to mind, feelings that continue to press themselves upon our hearts, tranquil feelings of peace and calm, and deep, abiding feelings of well-being are all examples of revelation from God to the soul. Learning to listen to those promptings is a key to understanding personal revelation, or the light within our minds and hearts.

Notes

1. Packer, "Candle of the Lord," 52.
2. Kimball, Conference Report, April 1977, 115.
3. Smith, *Teachings*, 247.
4. Packer, "Candle of the Lord," 53.
5. Smith, *Teachings*, 355.
6. Stoker, "Prophet Renews Friendships," 3.
7. Smith, *History of Joseph Smith*, 176–77.
8. Packer, *Ensign*, May 2000, 8.
9. Dunn, "Unity in the Faith," 62.
10. Smith, *Teachings*, 151.
11. Smith, *History of the Church*, 2:66.
12. Smith, *Teachings*, 137.
13. Packer, *Ensign*, November 1994, 60.
14. Packer, *Ensign*, "Candle of the Lord," 53.
15. Featherstone, *Man of Holiness*, 53.
16. Smith, *Teachings*, 214–15.
17. Smith, *History of the Church*, 5:4.
18. Packer, "Candle of the Lord," 53.
19. Packer, *Ensign*, November 1979, 21.
20. Young, *Journal of Discourses*, 3:205.
21. Packer, *Holy Temple*, 184.
22. Groberg, "What Is Your Mission?" 97–98.

CHAPTER 6

The Fruits of the Spirit

In a dream given to President Brigham Young, the Prophet Joseph Smith told him to teach the Saints to get and keep the Spirit of the Lord. The Prophet described the blessings that would result: "They can tell the Spirit of the Lord from all other spirits; it will whisper peace and joy to their souls, take malice, strife, and all evil from their hearts, and their whole desire will be to do good, bring forth righteousness and build up the kingdom of God."[1]

The fruits of the Spirit are associated with the gifts of the Spirit. They follow the law of the harvest—a natural outgrowth of the care and diligence given to sowing the seeds of the Spirit. The closer we are to the Spirit, the more easily the fruits of the Spirit can be harvested. Alma taught: "Now, if ye give place, that a seed may be planted in your heart, behold, . . . if ye do not cast it out by your unbelief, that ye will resist the Spirit of the Lord, behold, it will begin to swell within your breasts; and when you feel these swelling motions, ye will begin to say within yourselves—It must needs be that this is a good seed . . . for it beginneth to enlarge my soul; yea, it beginneth to enlighten my understanding, yea, it beginneth to be delicious to me" (Alma 32:28).

The fruits of the Spirit begin with the seed of faith, and the word *seed* can form an acronym for the harvest we can expect: the fruits of the Spirit will **s**well within us, **e**nlarge our souls, **e**nlighten our understanding, and be **d**elicious to us (Alma 32:28).

So what are the fruits or the blessings of the Spirit? The apostle Paul wrote: "The fruit of the Spirit is love, joy, peace, longsuffering, gentleness, goodness, faith, meekness, temperance [balance]" (Galatians 5:22–23). "For the fruit of the Spirit is in all goodness and righteousness and truth" (Ephesians 5:9). The Savior taught, "Put your trust in that Spirit which leadeth to do good—yea, to do justly, to walk humbly, to judge righteously; and this is my Spirit" (D&C 11:12), "for [God] is full of mercy, justice, grace and truth, and peace" (D&C 84:102).

Desire to Share

When the fruits of the Spirit are manifest, the love of God is present. Those who have the Lord's Spirit in their lives reflect God's love (1 John 4:8). This love and the fruit it bears are always accompanied by a sincere desire to share it with everyone. The fruits of the Spirit and the love of God motivate Church members to serve missions and in callings despite inconvenience. "This has been your feeling," the Prophet Joseph said to those about to embark on missions, "and caused you to forego the pleasure of home, that you might be a blessing to others, who are candidates for immortality, but strangers to truth; and for so doing, I pray that heaven's choicest blessings may rest upon you."[2] And they do!

The fruits of the Spirit and the love of God motivated the sons of Mosiah to serve for more than fourteen years as missionaries among their enemies: "Now they were desirous that salvation should be declared to every creature, for they could not bear that any human soul should perish; yea, even the very thoughts that any soul should endure endless torment did cause them to quake and tremble"(Mosiah 28:3).

When the candle of the Lord is lit in human hearts, those individuals delight to share that light with others. President Brigham Young said, "Suppose I should be called to preach the Gospel until my head is white, and my limbs become weak with age, until I go down into my grave, and never see my family and friends again in the flesh, would it be a sacrifice? No, but one of the greatest blessings that could be conferred upon mortal man, to have the privilege of calling thousands, and perhaps millions, from darkness to light, from the power of Satan and unrighteousness to the principles of truth and righteousness in the living God."[3]

This same desire moved the three Nephite apostles to ask to remain on the earth until the Second Coming to bring more souls unto Christ (3 Nephi 28:4–9). Because of his love for his fellowmen, John the Beloved had previously asked for this same privilege (D&C 7). The Savior honored their request and blessed them, saying, "For this cause ye shall have fulness of joy; and ye shall sit down in the kingdom of my Father; yea, your joy shall be full, even as the Father hath given me fulness of joy; and ye shall be even as I am, and I am even as the Father" (3 Nephi 28:10).

The desire to share the Spirit with others is most keenly felt for our own families. It caused Lehi, after he partook of the fruit of the tree of life, to beckon his family and to call them "with a loud voice that they should come unto [him], and partake of the fruit, which was desirable above all other fruit" (1 Nephi 8:15). Joseph Smith's father had a very similar dream in which he was also allowed to partake of this fruit. The first impression in his heart was, "I cannot eat this alone, I must bring my wife and children, that they may partake with me."[4]

The fruits of the Spirit are naturally attractive to spiritual people because they enjoyed them in the presence of our Heavenly Father before being born into mortality. People naturally hunger for what they once experienced.

President Harold B. Lee promised that if we would seek after and cultivate the fruits of the Spirit in our homes, the whole world would come knocking at our doors to have the same blessings: "I say to you Latter-day Saint mothers and fathers, if you will rise to the responsibility of teaching your children in the home—priesthood quorums preparing the fathers, the Relief Society the mothers—the day will soon be dawning when the whole world will come to our doors and will say, 'Show us your way that we may walk in your path.'"[5]

Sympathy of Spirit

When we are in the presence of individuals whose lives are filled with the fruit of the Spirit, who possess the peace that the Savior promised (John 14:27), we feel it. We know that they have been blessed by God and that even being in their presence is a blessing. We enjoy their companionship and look forward to being in their company. With such people we have what Parley P. Pratt called a "sympathetic affinity." Elder Pratt described how the fruit of the Spirit begins and eventually blossoms: "An intelligent being, in the image of God, possesses every organ, attribute, sense, sympathy, affection that is possessed by God Himself.

"But these are possessed by man, in his rudimental state, in a subordinate sense of the word. Or, in other words, these attributes are in embryo; and are to be gradually developed. They resemble a bud, a germ, which gradually develops into bloom, and then, by progress, produces the mature fruit, after its own kind.

"The gift of the Holy Ghost adapts itself to all these organs or attributes. It quickens all the intellectual faculties, increases, enlarges, expands and purifies all the natural passions and affections; and adapts them, by the gift of wisdom, to their lawful use. It inspires, develops, cultivates and matures all the fine-toned sympathies, joys, tastes, kindred feelings and affections of our nature. It inspires virtue, kindness, goodness, tenderness, gentleness and charity. It develops beauty of person, form and features. It tends to health, vigor, animation and social feeling. It invigorates all the faculties of the physical and intellectual man. It strengthens, and gives tone to the nerves. In short, it is, as it were, marrow to the bone, joy to the heart, light to the eyes, music to the ears, and life to the whole being.

"In the presence of such persons, one feels to enjoy the light of their countenances, as the genial rays of a sunbeam. Their very atmosphere diffuses a thrill, a warm glow of pure gladness and sympathy, to the heart and nerves of others who have kindred feelings, or sympathy of spirit. No matter if the parties are strangers, entirely unknown to each other in person or character; no matter if they have never spoken to each other, each will be apt to remark in his own mind, and perhaps exclaim, when referring to the interview—'O, what an atmosphere encircles that stranger! How my heart thrilled with pure and holy feelings in his presence! What confidence and sympathy he inspired! His countenance and spirit gave me more assurance than a thousand written recommendations, or introductory letters.' Such is the gift of the Holy Ghost, and such are its operations, when received through the lawful channel—the divine, eternal priesthood."[6]

Many journals of the early Saints describe just such feelings of kinship when they met the Prophet Joseph Smith. Amasa Lyman wrote: "Of the impressions produced I will here say, although there was nothing strange or different from other men in his personal appearance, yet when he grasped my hand in that cordial way, . . . I felt as one of old in the presence of the Lord; my strength seemed to be gone, so that it required an effort on my part to stand on my feet; but in all this there was no fear, but the serenity and peace of heaven pervaded my soul, and the still small voice of the spirit whispered its living testimony in the depths of my soul, where it has ever remained, that he was the man of God."[7]

This "sympathetic affinity," or feeling of peace in the presence of righteous people, was one of the gifts given to the Prophet Joseph Smith by the Lord to discern between those who had the Spirit and those who did not. The first time Joseph went up on the Hill Cumorah he saw the Book of Mormon plates, but he could not get them. Humbled by his inability to obtain the record, Joseph sought the Lord in prayer and was filled with the Spirit. Moroni appeared and gave Joseph strict instructions about how to prepare himself so that he could be entrusted with the record. Moroni showed him a vision of heaven and a vision of hell and said, "All this is shown, the good and the evil, the holy and impure, the glory of God and the power of darkness, that you may know hereafter the two powers and never be influenced or overcome by that wicked one."[8]

The Prophet later was taught that kindred spirits (those possessing the same inclination of spirit) would naturally be attracted to each other: "For intelligence cleaveth unto intelligence; wisdom receiveth wisdom; truth embraceth truth; virtue loveth virtue; light cleaveth unto light; mercy hath compassion on mercy and claimeth her own" (D&C 88:40).

Fruits of the Spirit

We can tell when the fruits of the Spirit are being manifest in our lives. Brigham Young University professor Don Norton has written that when we have the Spirit, we feel calm and happy. We feel full of light. Our minds are clear. Our bosoms burn with love for the Lord and for others. We feel generous. No one can offend us. We are very forgiving and kind. We feel confident in what we do. We don't mind anyone seeing what we are doing. We feel outgoing and anxious to be with others (especially family members). We are glad for others when they succeed. We want to make others happy, even those opposed to us. We bring out the best and say the best about others. We gladly and willingly perform Church work. We want to pray and read the scriptures. We want to keep all the Lord's commandments. We feel we have control of our appetites and emotions. We have controlled speech and no anger. We feel a deep desire to help others—usually in a way that no one else would know about. We speak and think only good about others. We feel sorrow when others have problems and sincerely desire to help them. We realize that our thoughts and our actions are open to God.[9]

Regeneration of Spirit

Having the Spirit with us leads to a second birth, a mighty change of heart (Alma 5:12), a spiritual regeneration. This new life begins at baptism and intensifies over time. "Being born again," Joseph Smith taught, "comes by the Spirit of God through ordinances."[10] For most members of the Church spiritual rebirth is a gradual process, experienced as they become "alive to one spiritual reality after another as they keep the commandments and seek to sanctify their souls."[11] "Mere compliance with the formality of the ordinance of baptism does not mean that a person has been born again. No one can be born again without baptism," Elder Bruce R. McConkie explained, but "the new birth takes place only for those who actually enjoy the gift or companionship of the Holy Ghost, . . . who have given themselves without restraint to the Lord."[12] To those who do, great rewards are realized, including happiness.

Happiness

"Happiness," Joseph Smith taught, "is the object and design of our existence."[13] We have been given the opportunity to come to mortality in order to prepare ourselves to receive unending joy: "Behold, all things have been done in the wisdom of him who knoweth all things. Adam fell that men might be; and men are, that they might have joy" (2 Nephi 2:24–25). Joy and happiness are truly "the object and design of our existence; and will be the end thereof, if we pursue the path that leads to it; and this path is virtue, uprightness, faithfulness, holiness, and keeping all the commandments of God."[14]

God is happy and dwells eternally in a place of great joy. His plan for our salvation is referred to in the Book of Mormon as the "great plan of happiness" (Alma 42:8). He knows what we need to do to go where he is. He has promised he will "wipe away all tears from [our] eyes; and there shall be no more death, neither sorrow, nor crying, neither shall there be any more pain" in his presence (Revelation 21:4).

But it is one thing to know about God, and another thing entirely to know him and experience the joy of having his Spirit. President Heber C. Kimball once remarked: "I am perfectly satisfied that my Father and my God is a cheerful, pleasant, lively, and good-natured Being. Why? Because I am cheerful, pleasant, lively, and good-natured when I have His Spirit. That is one reason why I know; and another is—the Lord said through Joseph Smith, 'I delight in a glad heart and a cheerful countenance' [see D&C 59:15]. That arises from the perfection of His attributes; He is a jovial, lively person, and a beautiful man."[15]

If that is what God's personality is like, would we expect his Spirit to be any different? Whenever the Spirit of God or the influence of the Holy Ghost is present, there are unmistakable spiritual benefits, including being edified (D&C 50:23). The manifestation of God's Spirit so completely revolutionizes our own spirits that feelings of gloom and loneliness depart. In their place, we are calm, happy, filled with light (D&C 50:24). The eternal fruit of the Spirit is never-ending happiness. Those who accept and follow the Savior's teachings are described in the scriptures as being happier than any other people on earth: "We lived after the manner of happiness" (2 Nephi 5:27); "there never was a happier time among the people" (Alma 50:23); "surely there could not be a happier people among all the people who had been created by the hand of God" (4 Nephi 1:16).

Hope

Another blessing of the Spirit is hope. The scriptures make it obvious that world conditions will worsen as we approach the time of the Savior's return to the earth. We are living in the times when peace has been taken from the earth and the devil has power over his own (D&C 1:35). Increasing wickedness and the technology to make it available instantaneously may hasten the time when "men's hearts shall fail them; for fear shall come upon all people" (D&C 88:91). The fear and worry associated with witnessing the rising tide of evil makes it an enormous challenge for the Saints to continue to hope. It will be increasingly important for us to keep the light of hope burning brightly and to look forward to the fulfillment of all the promises the Lord holds out to his faithful Saints. He has assured us that despite the challenges we can "be of good cheer, and do not fear, for I the Lord am with you, and will stand by you" (D&C 68:6). Moreover, he has promised, "Ye cannot bear all things now; nevertheless, be of good cheer, for I will lead you along. The kingdom is yours and the blessings thereof are yours, and the riches of eternity are yours" (D&C 78:18).

The absolute proof that Christ has overcome all things was the showing of his resurrected body. He has overcome everything that causes us fear, including death itself! That is why Mormon wrote to Moroni: "Be faithful in Christ; . . . may Christ lift thee up, and may his sufferings and death, and the showing his body unto our fathers, and his mercy and long-suffering, and the hope of his glory and of eternal life, rest in your mind forever" (Moroni 9:25).

Hope, in the spiritual sense, comes from our faith in Jesus Christ (Ether 12:4). It is the consummate companion of those who walk with Christ. Eternal hope and the assurance that God understands perfectly what we are going through are essential to our happiness. Elder Dean L. Larsen observed, "It is quite possible that one of the greatest challenges facing the Lord's people in the years ahead will be to cope with the coming difficulties without becoming despondent and pessimistic about the final outcome of things. . . . The Lord also made it clear that those who understand the nature of the times, and who keep themselves informed of and in harmony with his words, will have reason for optimism and hope."[16]

Through the Prophet Joseph Smith this great assurance about the future has been revealed: "For behold, again I say unto you that if ye will enter in by the way, and receive the Holy Ghost, it will show unto you all things what ye should do" (2 Nephi 32:5). Citing this passage, President Boyd K. Packer declared, "We need not live in fear of the future. We have every reason to rejoice and little reason to fear. If we follow the promptings of the Spirit, we will be safe, whatever the future holds. We will be shown what to do."[17]

Edification and Enlightenment

Whenever the Spirit is present, spirituality, friendship, and lives will always be improved. The Lord said that his Spirit would enlighten our minds (D&C 6:15). He promised that when we teach with his Spirit, "he that preacheth and he that receiveth, understand one another, and both are edified and rejoice together." He also warned that anything that does not edify "is not of God, and is darkness," because "that which is of God is light; and he that receiveth light, and continueth in God, receiveth more light" (D&C 50:22–24).

The word *edify* means "to build." "It comes from the Latin *aedificare*, which means to instruct or improve spirituality, and the Latin word *aedes*, which means 'temple' or 'house,'" wrote Randall L. Hall. "Religious education, in a very real way, is the process of constructing, as it were, living temples. For, as the apostle Paul asked, 'Know ye not that ye are the temple of God, and that the Spirit of God dwelleth in you?' (1 Corinthians 3:16)."[18]

The Lord has promised that his Spirit will both enlighten and edify us: "Verily, verily, I say unto you, I will impart unto you of my Spirit, which shall enlighten your mind, which shall fill your soul with joy" (D&C 11:13).

Peace

Still another sweet fruit of the Spirit is peace. There is so little peace to be found in our world, but the promise of the Savior is "Fear not, little children, for you are mine, and I have overcome the world, and you are of them that my Father hath given me" (D&C 50:41). "These things I have spoken unto you, that in me ye might have peace. In the world ye shall have tribulation: but be of good cheer; I have overcome the world" (John 16:33).

When Oliver Cowdery heard about Joseph Smith's seeing an angel and receiving an ancient record, he prayed to know if it was true. He received a peaceful assurance it was. A short time later, the Lord reminded him of the witness of peace that had been borne to his soul, asking, "Did I not speak peace to your mind concerning the matter? What greater witness can you have than from God?" (D&C 6:23). Inner peace is one of the greatest witnesses that can be experienced.

God has promised this peace to all who seek after him: "Learn of me, and listen to my words; walk in the meekness of my Spirit, and you shall have peace in me" (D&C 19:23). True peace can be found only in him (Moroni 10:32–33). That was the message of the angels who heralded his birth: "And suddenly there was with the angel a multitude of the heavenly host praising God, and saying, Glory to God in the highest; and on earth, peace" (JST Luke 2:13–14).

Many people wonder if we will ever see peace on the earth. Conferences are held to broker peace between nations, and prayers are said for world peace. The Savior has promised that when he returns to the earth to begin his millennial reign, there will finally be peace on earth, and "all thy children shall be taught of the Lord; and great shall be the peace of thy children" (3 Nephi 22:13). Our children can have peace when they are "taught of the Lord"—meaning they need to be taught about him and be taught by the Spirit.

President John Taylor said, "Peace is the gift of God. Do you want peace? Go to God. Do you want peace in your families? Go to God. Do you want peace to brood over your families? If you do, live your religion, and the very peace of God will dwell and abide with you, for that is where peace comes from."[19]

Truly there is no greater peace than that which comes from Christ: "Peace I leave with you, my peace I give unto you: not as the world giveth, give I unto you. Let not your heart be troubled, neither let it be afraid" (John 14:27). Perhaps the greatest example in the Book of Mormon of the peace and joy coming from the Spirit was when Christ knelt with and prayed for the people as recorded in 3 Nephi: "And no tongue can speak, neither can there be written by any man, neither can the hearts of men conceive so great and marvelous things as we both saw and heard Jesus speak; and no one can conceive of the joy which filled our souls at the time we heard him pray for us unto the Father" (3 Nephi 17:17).

After suffering for five months in deplorable conditions in Liberty Jail during the winter of 1838–39, the Prophet Joseph pleaded with God for relief. The Lord spoke these comforting words to his prophet: "My son, peace be unto thy soul; thine adversity and thine afflictions shall be but a small moment; And then, if thou endure it well, God shall exalt thee on high; thou shalt triumph over all thy foes" (D&C 121:7–8).

The Spirit often sends revelation to comfort us. When Alma and his people were taken captive by their enemies, the word of the Lord came to them in their afflictions: "Lift up your heads and be of good comfort, for I know of the covenant which ye have made unto me; and I will covenant with my people and deliver them out of bondage. And I will also ease the burdens which are put upon your shoulders, that even you cannot feel them upon your backs" (Mosiah 24:13–14).

President Brigham Young gave us his testimony of how comforting the peace of God can be in times of trouble:

"You that have not passed through the trials, and persecutions, and drivings, with this people, from the beginning, but have only read them, or heard some of them related, may think how awful they were to endure, and wonder that the Saints survived them at all. The thought of it makes your hearts sink within you, your brains reel, and your bodies tremble, and you are ready to exclaim, 'I could not have endured it.' I have been in the heat of it, and I never felt better in all my life; *I never felt the peace and power of the Almighty more copiously poured upon me than in the keenest part of our trials*. They appeared nothing to me. I hear people talk about their troubles, their sore privations, and the great sacrifices they have made for the Gospel's sake. It never was a sacrifice to me. Anything I can do or suffer in the cause of the Gospel, is only like dropping a pin into the sea; the blessings, gifts, powers, honour, joy, truth, salvation, glory, immortality, and eternal lives, as far outswell anything I can do in return for such precious gifts, as the great ocean exceeds in expansion, bulk, and weight, the pin that I drop into it."[20]

President Lorenzo Snow expressed a similar testimony: "Now, Latter-day Saints, how is it with us? We have received the Gospel. We have received the kingdom of God, established on the earth. We have had trouble; we have been persecuted. We were driven from Ohio; we were driven from Missouri; we were driven from Nauvoo; and once we were driven for a time from this beautiful city [Salt Lake City]. Many have lost thousands of dollars; lost their homes and all they had, and some of the brethren have seen their wives and children lay down their lives because of the hardships they had to experience during these changes, these persecutions, these revolutions and these drivings. The people have looked with astonishment at the willingness of the Latter-day Saints to suffer these things. Why do we do this? Why do we adhere to these principles that have caused us at times so much grief and sacrifice? What is it that enables us to endure these persecutions and still rejoice? It is because we have had revelations from the Almighty; because He has spoken to us in our souls and has given to us the Holy Ghost, which is a principle of revelation wherever it exists and is promised to every man, as in the days of the former Apostles, who will believe, repent of his sins and be immersed in water for the remission of them by those who have the authority from the Lord to administer this ordinance. Jesus, when he was among the children of men, said that He would build His church upon this principle of revelation and the gates of hell should not prevail against it."[21]

A Peaceable Walk with Others

Choice blessings are reserved for peacemakers. "Blessed are all the peacemakers, for they shall be called the children of God" (3 Nephi 12:9). Those filled with the love of God receive peace in their lives and no longer find it necessary to argue or contend with others: "And it came to pass that there was no contention in the land, because of the love of God which did dwell in the hearts of the people" (4 Nephi 1:15). Peaceable followers of Christ have the privilege of entering "into the rest of the Lord" in this life and "shall rest with him in heaven" in the next (Moroni 7:3).

The Prophet Joseph demonstrated how being filled with the Spirit enables us to have a "peaceable walk" with others (Moroni 7:4). He urged the Saints to avoid criticizing one another: "I charged the Saints not to follow the example of the adversary in accusing the brethren, and said, 'If you do not accuse each other, God will not accuse you. If you have no accuser you will enter heaven, and if you will follow the revelations and instructions which God gives you through me, I will take you into heaven as my back load. If you will not accuse me, I will not accuse you. If you will throw a cloak of charity over my sins, I will over yours—for charity covereth a multitude of sins. What many people call sin is not sin.'"[22]

Joseph once taught a woman how to deal with personal injury and not lose the Spirit or destroy a relationship. Jesse W. Crosby recorded:

"I went one day to the Prophet with a sister. She had a charge to make against one of the brethren for scandal. When her complaint had been heard the Prophet asked her if she was quite sure that what the brother had said of her was utterly untrue.

"She was quite sure that it was.

"He then told her to think no more about it, for it could not harm her. If untrue it could not live, but the truth will survive. Still she felt that she should have some redress.

"Then he offered her his method of dealing with such cases for himself. When an enemy had told a scandalous story about him, which had often been done, before he rendered judgment he paused and let his mind run back to the time and place and setting of the story to see if he had not by some unguarded word or act laid the block on which the story was built. If he found that he had done so, he said that in his heart he then forgave his enemy, and felt thankful that he had received warning of a weakness that he had not known he possessed.

"Then he said to the sister that he would have her to do the same: search her memory thoroughly and see if she had not herself unconsciously laid the foundation for the scandal that annoyed her.

"The sister thought deeply for a few moments and then confessed that she believed she had.

"Then the Prophet told her that in her heart she could forgive that brother who had risked his own good name and her friendship to give her this clearer view of herself.

"The sister thanked her advisor and went away in peace."[23]

This peaceful approach to problem solving is radically different from what we see in the world. The natural man refuses to submit—to God or to others. Truly God's ways are much higher than ours: "For as the heavens are higher than the earth, so are my ways higher than your ways, and my thoughts than your thoughts" (Isaiah 55:9).

Charity, the Greatest of All

The Prophet Joseph taught that "love is one of the chief characteristics of Deity, and ought to be manifested by those who aspire to be the sons of God."[24] He also said, "Nothing is so much calculated to lead people to forsake sin as to take them by the hand, and watch over them with tenderness. When persons manifest the least kindness and love to me, O what power it has over my mind, while the opposite course has a tendency to harrow up all the harsh feelings and depress the human mind."[25]

The Book of Mormon explains that charity is the pure love of

Christ (Moroni 7:47). It is "the highest, noblest, strongest kind of love, not merely affection."[26] Charity is God's perfect love for his children (Ether 12:34). It is the everlasting love that gave Jesus Christ the ability to do His Father's will—to suffer the demands of justice and atone for all mankind—thus making exaltation and eternal life possible for all Heavenly Father's children (1 Nephi 19:9; Mosiah 15:8–9; Alma 42:15; Moroni 8:17; Moses 1:39).

The Lord commanded that all should have charity and taught that those without it cannot inherit the celestial kingdom (2 Nephi 26:30; Ether 12:34; Moroni 10:21). Those who possess charity become the sons and daughters of God, become like Christ, and will be "lifted up at the last day and enter into his rest" (Alma 13:29).

The Savior has commanded all his disciples to have charity: "A new commandment I give unto you, That ye love one another; as I have loved you, that ye also love one another. By this shall all men know that ye are my disciples, if ye have love one to another" (John 13:34–35). Charity is the enabling power that permits mortals to keep fully the two great commandments in the law: "Thou shalt love the Lord thy God with all thy heart, and with all thy soul, and with all thy mind. . . . And . . . thou shalt love thy neighbour as thyself" (Matthew 22:37, 39).

In his dream of the tree of life, the prophet Lehi tasted the fruit of the tree, which represented the love of God as expressed in the atonement of Jesus Christ (1 Nephi 8:10; 11:22, 25). Lehi described the love of God as being the most desirable of all things. He said it is "sweet, above all," "white, to exceed all the whiteness" (1 Nephi 8:11), and "desirable above all other fruit" (1 Nephi 8:12). It has "beauty . . . far beyond . . . all beauty," is "precious above all" (1 Nephi 11:8–9), and is "most joyous to the soul" (1 Nephi 11:23). The prophet Alma described the love he felt at the time of his forgiveness as "pure above all that is pure" (Alma 32:42).

The love of God makes one happy (1 Nephi 8:10) and gives one an overwhelming desire to invite others (family, friends, and even enemies) to partake of it also (1 Nephi 8:13–17; Enos 1:9, 11; Alma 36:24). The Prophet Joseph said, "A man filled with the love of God, is not content with blessing his family alone, but ranges through the whole world, anxious to bless the whole human race."[27]

Faith in Jesus Christ and hope (anchored in his assurance of eternal life) leads to charity (Moroni 10:20), and charity leads us to Christ (Ether 12:28). No mortal can love the Savior or his fellowmen as God does unless God reveals that love to him (Alma 5:26). Charity is revealed to those who seek it diligently. It comes to those who "pray unto the Father with all the energy of heart, that [they] may be filled with this love," and it is bestowed upon "all who are true followers of . . . Jesus Christ" (Moroni 7:48). Those who receive the gift of charity are filled with such pure love that they would give everything they are or ever hope to be to regain the Father's presence and enjoy permanently what they experienced at the time they were cloaked with charity.

Charity is the greatest of all the spiritual gifts (1 Corinthians 13:2, 8). It helps us to "always abound in good works" (Alma 7:24). The Savior told Joseph Smith, "Let thy bowels also be full of charity towards all men" (D&C 121:45). Daniel Tyler, an associate of the Prophet Joseph, recorded an incident illustrating how Joseph exercised charity towards others:

"A man who had stood high in the Church while in Far West was taken down with chills or ague and fever. While his mind as well as body was weak, disaffected parties soured his mind and persuaded him to leave the Saints and go with them. He gave some testimony against the Prophet. . . . [After leaving the Church and moving from Missouri to Illinois] he went to work chopping cordwood to obtain means to take himself and family to Nauvoo, and provide a present to the injured man of God [Joseph Smith] if, peradventure, [Joseph] would forgive and permit him to return to the fold as a private member. He felt that there was salvation nowhere else for him, and if that was denied him, all was lost as far as he was concerned.

"He started with a sorrowful heart and downcast look. While [he was] on the way, the Lord told Brother Joseph he was coming. The Prophet looked out of the window and saw him coming up the street. As soon as he turned to open the gate, the Prophet sprang up from his chair and ran and met him in the yard, exclaiming, 'O Brother, how glad I am to see you!' He caught him around the neck, and both wept like children."[28]

The atonement of Jesus Christ is the greatest manifestation of charity ever known. Elder Jeffrey R. Holland wrote: "The greater definition of 'the pure love of Christ' . . . is not what we as Christians try but largely fail to demonstrate toward others but rather what Christ totally succeeded in demonstrating toward us. *True* charity has been known only once. It is shown perfectly and purely in Christ's unfailing, ultimate, and atoning love for us. It is Christ's love for us that 'suffereth long, and is kind.' . . . It is Christ's love for us that 'beareth all things, . . . endureth all things.' It is as demonstrated in Christ that 'charity never faileth.' It is that charity—his pure love for us—without which we would be nothing, hopeless, of all men and women most miserable. Truly, those found possessed of the blessings of his love at the last day—the Atonement, the Resurrection, eternal life, eternal promise—surely it shall be well with them.

"This does not in any way minimize the commandment that we are to try to acquire this kind of love for one another. We should 'pray unto the Father with all the energy of heart, that [we] may be filled with this love' [1 Corinthians 13:4–5, 7–8; Moroni 7:48]. We should try to be more constant and unfailing, more longsuffering and kind, less envious and puffed up in our relationships with others. As Christ lived so should we live, and as Christ loved so should we love. But the '*pure* love of Christ' Mormon spoke of is precisely that—Christ's love. With that divine gift, that redeeming bestowal, we have everything; without it we have nothing and ultimately are nothing, except in the end 'devils [and] angels to a devil' [2 Nephi 9:9]."[29]

Elder Orson F. Whitney shared an event from the Prophet Joseph's life demonstrating his example of feeling charity and compassion, even toward bitter enemies: "He and some of his brethren were lying in a dungeon, Liberty jail, Missouri, during the winter of 1838–9, after the Saints, fifteen thousand men, women and children, had been driven from the state of Missouri. These brethren were treated with great cruelty in prison. It is said that the depravity of their jailers descended so low that they even cooked human flesh, taken from the body of a [man] who had been killed, and offered it to these prisoners to eat; and the

Prophet, warned by the Lord, told his brethren not to partake of it. It was in the midst of these circumstances that one of the brethren was asked to pray; and he prayed that God would damn the men who were treating them thus cruelly. . . . The Prophet then told him, 'You yourself will yet see the day when you will pity these very men who are inflicting these injuries upon you. God has shown to me in vision the sufferings of the ungodly, and I had to pray to Him to close the vision when I saw the terrible judgments that would come upon the wicked.' The Prophet taught the principle of patient submission to wrong. And it is this that lifts men up above other men."[30]

Bounteous Harvest

The Lord invites us to reap a bounteous harvest of the fruits of the Spirit. The fruits of the Spirit, including regeneration of spirit, happiness, hope, edification, enlightenment, peace, peaceable walk with others, and charity, as well as many others, are available to all. What the Lord said about missionary work and working hard to gather Israel could also be said about the effort we should expend to gather the fruits of the Spirit: "Behold, the field is white already to harvest; therefore, whoso desireth to reap let him thrust in his sickle with his might, and reap while the day lasts, that he may treasure up for his soul everlasting salvation in the kingdom of God" (D&C 12:3).

Notes

1. Elden J. Watson, comp., Manuscript History of Brigham Young 1846–1847, 529–30, as cited in Romney, Conference Report, April 1944, 141.
2. Smith, *Teachings*, 174–75.
3. Young, *Journal of Discourses*, 1:313–14.
4. Smith, *History of Joseph Smith*, 51.
5. Lee, Conference Report, October 1964, 87.
6. Pratt, *Key to the Science of Theology*, 100–102.

7. "Autobiographical Sketch of Amasa M. Lyman," *Millennial Star* 27 (1865): 473, as cited in Smith, *History of the Church*, 1:332–33.
8. Pratt, *Voice of Warning*, 85.
9. Norton, "I Have a Question," 32–33.
10. Smith, *History of the Church*, 3:392.
11. McConkie, "What Does It Mean to Be Born Again?" 36.
12. McConkie, *Mormon Doctrine*, 101.
13. Smith, *Teachings*, 255.
14. Smith, *Teachings*, 255–56.
15. Kimball, *Journal of Discourses*, 4:222.
16. Larsen, "'Prepare Ye for That Which Is to Come,'" 1.
17. Packer, *Ensign*, May 2000, 8.
18. Hall, "Preeminence of Teaching," 4.
19. Taylor, *Journal of Discourses*, 10:56.
20. Young, *Journal of Discourses*, 1:313.
21. Snow, Conference Report, April 1900, 2–3.
22. Smith, *Teachings*, 193.
23. Jesse W. Crosby, "Stories from the Notebook of Martha Cox, Grandmother of Fern Cox Anderson," Church Archives; or Lee C. LaFayette, "Recollections of Joseph Smith," Church Archives, as cited in Andrus and Andrus, *They Knew the Prophet*, 162–63.
24. Smith, *History of the Church*, 4:227.
25. Smith, *Teachings*, 240.
26. LDS Bible Dictionary, 632.
27. Smith, *History of the Church*, 4:227.
28. Dahl and Cannon, *Teachings of Joseph Smith*, 271.
29. Holland, *Christ and the New Covenant*, 336–37.
30. Whitney, "Three Great Teachers," in Stuy, *Collected Discourses*, vol. 5.

CHAPTER 7

"Be Still and Know That I Am God"

The scriptures make it clear that the Lord will hasten his work in the last days (D&C 88:73) and that we are living in those days (2 Nephi 12:2). There is so much to do, so many places to be, and so much to see. We lead very busy lives. Our lives are cluttered with calendars, to-do lists, and obligations. We have more clocks and less free time. Fax machines, cell phones, laptop computers, and pagers do not, contrary to advertisers' promises, make life simpler. They often make it more complex because they keep us in touch with to-do lists twenty-four hours a day.

President Wilford Woodruff related an interview he had with the Prophet Joseph Smith: "In the night vision I saw him at the door of the temple in heaven. He came to me and spoke to me. He said he could not stop to talk with me because he was in a hurry. The next man I met was Father Smith [Joseph Smith Sr.]; he could not talk with me because he was in a hurry. I met half a dozen brethren who had held high positions on earth, and none of them could stop to talk with me because they were in a hurry. I was much astonished. By and by I saw the Prophet again and I got the privilege of asking him a question.

"'Now,' said I, 'I want to know why you are in a hurry. I have been in a hurry all my life; but I expected my hurry would be over when I got into the kingdom of heaven, if I ever did.'

"Joseph replied: 'I will tell you, Brother Woodruff. Every dispensation that has had the priesthood on the earth and has gone into the celestial kingdom has had a certain amount of work to do to prepare to go to the earth with the Savior when he goes to reign on the earth. Each dispensation has had ample time to do this work. We have not. We are the last dispensation, and so much work has to be done, and we need to be in a hurry in order to accomplish it.'"[1]

Too Busy

We are convinced that we have no time, when in fact, the Lord has blessed us with so many labor-saving devices that we actually have more free time than any people who have ever lived. Ironically, so many things occupy our minds and our time that to turn our hearts to the Lord, we may have to learn to turn our hearts away from other things. The adversary makes us think that we must be more busy and more burdened than we ought to be. We could make the mistake of assuming that *busy-ness* is the same as *progress*. The two are not always equal. In fact, our society in some ways is moving forward—backwards! We are making rapid strides forward in so many ways, yet in others, we seem to be going backwards. We are surrounded by technological giants and ethical infants. Just as there was no room for Christ in the world of his day, so there seems to be little room for his teachings in today's world.

If some of us feel that personal revelation is elusive, could it be because, like our society, we are in just too much of a hurry? What Joseph Smith told Wilford Woodruff is absolutely correct—there is much to do in this last dispensation, and we have to hurry to get it all done, but there is a difference between being part of the Lord's work while it is being hastened in its day and just being in haste. President Boyd K. Packer observed, "I fear this supernal gift [revelation from the Holy Ghost] is being obscured by programs and activities and schedules and so many meetings. There are so many places to go, so many things to do in this noisy world. We can be too busy to pay attention to the promptings of the Spirit."[2]

Consider what the Prophet Joseph said about spending time with spiritual things: "The things of God are of deep import; and time, and experience, and careful and ponderous and solemn thoughts can only find them out. Thy mind, O man! if thou wilt lead a soul [including your own soul!] unto salvation, must stretch as high as the utmost heavens, and search into and contemplate the darkest abyss, and the broad expanse of eternity."[3]

Could some of the frenetic, busy-ness in society be one way the adversary prevents us from slowing down enough to spend time doing things that matter most? We are constantly "doing" things. But are we really experiencing the things of most importance? In the April 1994 general conference, Elder Neal A. Maxwell asked, "Given the gravity of current conditions, would parents be willing to give up just one outside thing, giving that time and talent instead to the family?"[4] Being busy, managing time, and trying to squeeze every last second out of life has become prestigious. But if we are too busy, we may be missing some of the sweeter spiritual experiences simply because the Lord may not be able to reach us. In God's eyes, a "quiet spirit" is worth a great price (1 Peter 3:4).

Not in Haste

Busy-ness can never be used as an excuse for disobedience to God's commandments. In 1834, the Prophet Joseph recorded in his journal: "No month ever found me more busily engaged than November; but as my life consisted of activity and unyielding exertions, I made this my rule: When the Lord commands, do it."[5]

Life may be busy, but communion with God cannot be rushed or hurried. Many times in the scriptures the Prince of Peace has counseled the Saints to do things well but not to run about in haste or confusion:

"Let the work of the gathering be not in haste, nor by flight; but let it be done as it shall be counseled by the elders of the church at the conferences" (D&C 58:56).

"And now, behold, this is the will of the Lord your God concerning his saints, that they should assemble themselves together . . . , not in haste, lest there should be confusion, which bringeth pestilence" (D&C 63:24).

"Let these things be done in their time, but not in haste; and observe to have all things prepared before you" (D&C 101:72).

"He that believeth shall not make haste" (Isaiah 28:16).

"See that all these things are done in wisdom and order; for it is not requisite that a man should run faster than he has strength. And again, it is expedient that he should be diligent, that thereby he might win the prize; therefore, all things must be done in order" (Mosiah 4:27).

When others feel we are too busy, they hesitate to add to our burdens by asking us for help or for some other involvement in their lives. That can lead to lost opportunities to deepen relationships. Consider what could happen if, in our Church callings, we gave the impression that we are too busy to help. The Savior, whose three-year ministry surely pressed him for time, never gave the impression that he was too busy to visit, or sit with, or eat with those who needed his counsel. He also taught, by example, the necessity of occasionally spending some quiet time alone (Matthew 14:23; John 6:15).

Time to Meditate and Ponder

In 1832, when the Prophet Joseph Smith and others were traveling from Indiana toward New Albany, Ohio, they were delayed when their coach stopped, and the driver stepped down. Joseph described what happened next: "The horses became frightened, and while going at full speed Bishop [Newel K.] Whitney attempted to jump out of the coach, but having his coat fast, caught his foot in the wheel and had his leg and foot broken in several places; at the same time I jumped out unhurt."[6] Joseph stayed with Bishop Whitney at a public house until he was well enough to travel. Bishop Whitney was bedfast for several weeks. Joseph had time to walk and ponder. There was no pressure from duties and no one asking him questions or seeking his counsel. For the first time in years he had a real chance to be alone. Sometime during their stay, Joseph wrote an intimate letter to Emma, his wife. His personal struggle for forgiveness of his weaknesses and the assurance he received from the Lord is touching and gives us a glimpse of the peace that can come when we take time to commune with God:

"I have visited a grove which is just back of the town almost every day where I can be secluded from the eyes of any mortal and there give vent to all the feeling[s] of my heart in meditation and pray[er]. I have called to mind all the past moments of my life and am left to mourn and shed tears of sorrow for my folly in suffering the adversary of my soul to have so much power over me as he has had in times past, but God is merciful and has forgiven my sins, and I rejoice that he sendeth forth the Comforter unto as many as believe and humble themselves before him."[7]

The revelation of comfort and consolation that Joseph received came when he had time to be still. Joseph later said that "the manifestations of the gift of the Holy Ghost; the ministering of angels; or the development of the power, majesty or glory of God were very seldom manifested publicly, and that generally to the people of God; as to the Israelites; but most generally when angels have come, or God has revealed himself, it has been to individuals in private—in their chamber—in the wilderness or fields; and that generally without noise or tumult."[8]

The quiet meditation of the soul is an important way to attune ourselves to the voice of the Spirit. Impressions are more easily detected when we find time to ponder deeply. President David O. McKay said: "I think we pay too little attention to the value of meditation, a principle of devotion. In our worship there are two elements: One is spiritual communion arising from our own meditation; the other, instruction from others, particularly from those who have authority to guide and instruct us. Of the two, the more profitable introspectively is the meditation. Meditation is the language of the soul. It is defined as 'a form of private devotion, or spiritual exercise, consisting in deep, continued reflection on some religious theme.' Meditation is a form of prayer. . . .

"Meditation is one of the most secret, most sacred doors through which we pass into the presence of the Lord. Jesus set the example for us. As soon as he was baptized and received the Father's approval, 'This is my Beloved Son, in whom I am well pleased,' Jesus repaired to what is now know as the mount of temptation. I like to think of it as the mount of *meditation* where, during the forty days of fasting, he communed with himself and his Father, and contemplated upon the responsibility of his great mission."[9]

Taking time for meditation and serious thought was one of President McKay's most frequently repeated messages to Church leaders. Meditation truly is "one of the . . . most sacred doors through which we pass into the presence of the Lord." President Harold B. Lee shared what he had heard President McKay teach about receiving promptings and impressions from the Spirit. He said that "when we are relaxed in a private room we are more susceptible to those things [spiritual promptings]; and that so far as he was concerned, his best thoughts come after he gets up in the morning and is relaxed and thinking about the duties of the day; that impressions come more clearly, as if it were to hear a voice. Those impressions are right. If we are worried about something and upset in our feelings, the inspiration does not come. If we so live that our minds are free from worry and our conscience is clear and our feelings are right toward one another, the operation of the Spirit of the Lord upon our spirit is as real as when we pick up the telephone; but when they come, we must be brave enough to take the suggested actions."[10]

That early morning stillness of the soul can be spiritually energizing. Perhaps that is one reason the Lord counseled: "Retire to thy bed early, that ye may not be weary: arise early, that your bodies and your minds may be invigorated" (D&C 88:124).

Inner Peace

The Prophet Joseph learned many valuable lessons about revelation while he was translating the Book of Mormon. One of the most important was that he had to be at peace with others around him in order to hear and feel the whisperings of the Spirit. "He had to trust in God," David Whitmer wrote. "He could not translate unless he was humble and possessed the right feelings towards everyone. To illustrate so you can see: One morning when he was getting ready to continue the translation, something went wrong about the house and he was put out about it. Something that Emma, his wife, had done. Oliver and I went upstairs, and Joseph came up soon after to continue the translation but he could not do anything. He could not translate a single syllable. He went downstairs, out into the orchard, and made supplication to the Lord; was gone about an hour, came back to the house, and asked Emma's forgiveness and then came upstairs where we were and then the translation went on all right. He could do nothing save he was humble and faithful."[11]

Parley P. Pratt, an apostle who had been in the School of the Prophets taught by Joseph Smith, wrote a book to help people understand that theology (the study of what God is like and how we can become like him) can be studied in a logical way, much like a science. The title of his book was, therefore, *Key to the Science of Theology*. In his chapter on dreams as a means of revelation, Elder Pratt described how the inner calm of the body and the soul can lead to greater revelation from the Lord:

"In all dispensations God has revealed many important instructions and warnings to men by means of dreams.

"When the outward organs of thought and perception are released from their activity, the nerves unstrung, and the whole of mortal humanity lies hushed in quiet slumbers, in order to renew its strength and vigor, it is then that the spiritual organs are at liberty, in a certain degree, to assume their wonted functions, to recall some faint outlines, some confused and half-defined recollections, of that heavenly world, and those endearing scenes of their former estate, from which they have descended in order to obtain and mature a tabernacle of flesh. Their kindred spirits, their guardian angels then hover about them with the fondest affection, the most anxious solicitude. Spirit communes with spirit, thought meets thought, soul blends with soul, in all the raptures of mutual, pure, and eternal love.

"In this situation, the spiritual organs are susceptible of converse with Deity, or of communion with angels, and the spirits of just men made perfect."[12]

"Be Still"

The voice of the Spirit is a quiet one that must be felt. When our hearts and minds are at peace and we are quiet inside, we can feel and receive promptings. That is why busy-ness in our lives may prevent us from feeling the Spirit. To sense and understand promptings, the soul must be still. When there is an inner calm, we can feel the influence of the Spirit most strongly. "Be still," the Lord counseled, "and know that I am God" (D&C 101:16). There is a difference between just being "quiet" and being "still." We come to know his voice best when we are still in our souls. The Prophet Joseph said that when the Holy Ghost falls upon us, "it is calm and serene."[13]

Even when there is chaos and tumult or conflict all around us, we can still tune our souls to the Lord's Spirit, which speaks to the depth of our innermost soul. After the tremendous physical upheavals and destructions accompanying the Savior's death, the Nephites in ancient America required a few minutes of inner listening before they could understand the Savior's words, but his voice pierced their hearts:

"And it came to pass that while they were thus conversing one with another, they heard a voice as if it came out of heaven; and they cast their eyes round about, for they understood not the voice which they heard; and it was not a harsh voice, neither was it a loud voice; nevertheless, and notwithstanding it being a small voice it did pierce them that did hear to the center, insomuch that there was no part of their frame that it did not cause to quake; yea, it did pierce them to the very soul, and did cause their hearts to burn" (3 Nephi 11:3).

The voice of the Spirit whispers to our souls, almost as if someone were standing behind us softly whispering: "Thine ears shall hear a word behind thee, saying, This is the way, walk ye in it, when ye turn to the right hand, and when ye turn to the left" (Isaiah 30:21). Yet it pierces us to the center with confidence and assurance. When John the Baptist, as a resurrected being, appeared to Joseph Smith and Oliver Cowdery, they said, "His voice, though mild, pierced to the center" (Joseph Smith–History, footnote, paragraph 5).

Finding Inner Calm

Everything from books and videos to physical exercises have been promoted as having the best, most reliable method of achieving inner peace. But the Lord has given us some very simple ways to get close to the Spirit. Here are six of them:

Personal prayer. Prayer time is like an oasis of solitude. The Savior always took time to find a place where he could be alone and pray. "And when he had sent the multitudes away, he went up into a mountain apart to pray: and when the evening was come, he was there alone" (Matthew 14:23).

Paul wrote Timothy that the primary reason he exhorted people to pray was to help them "lead a quiet and peaceable life in all godliness and honesty. For this is good and acceptable in the sight of God our Saviour" (1 Timothy 2:2–3).

President James E. Faust wrote about the sacredness of personal prayer: "An important part of the spiritual being of all of us is the quiet and sacred part from which we may feel a sanctification in our lives. It is that part of us wherein no other soul intrudes. It is that part of us that permits us to come close to the divine, both in and out of this world. This portion of our beings is reserved only for ourselves and our Creator; we open the portals thereof when we pray."[14]

The Savior counseled us to pray thoughtfully: "Verily I say unto you, my friends, I leave these sayings with you to ponder in your hearts, with this commandment which I give unto you, that ye shall call upon me while I am near—Draw near unto me and I will draw near unto you; seek me diligently and ye shall find me; ask, and ye shall receive; knock, and it shall be opened unto you. Whatsoever ye ask the Father in my name it shall be given unto you, that is expedient for you" (D&C 88:62–64).

Scripture study. With the myriad of commentaries and other books about scripture available to us, it is possible to be forever reading what others have said about the scriptures without ever reading the words of the Lord for ourselves. But by reading the word of God and asking him for enlightenment, for help in understanding what portion of his word belongs to us, we can receive promptings and insight from the Holy Ghost. When we read the words of the Lord, the Spirit can confirm in our hearts the truth of what we learn. That is an important way the voice of the Lord can speak to each of us: "These words are not of men nor of man, but of me; . . . and by my power you can read them one to another. . . . Wherefore, you can testify that you have heard my voice, and know my words" (D&C 18:34–36). As we do, we are also blessed with his Spirit: "And behold, whosoever believeth on my words, them will I visit with the manifestation of my Spirit" (D&C 5:16).

Elder Carlos Asay said scripture study is like an interview with Deity: "I fear that many of us rush about from day to day taking for granted the holy scriptures. We scramble to honor appointments with physicians, lawyers, and businessmen. Yet we think nothing of postponing interviews with Deity—postponing scripture study. Little wonder we develop anemic souls and lose our direction in living. How much better it would be if we planned and held sacred fifteen or twenty minutes a day for reading the scriptures. Such interviews with Deity would help us recognize his voice and enable us to receive guidance in all of our affairs. We must look to God through the scriptures."[15]

Elder Bruce R. McConkie noted that "we are so wound up in programs and statistics and trends, in properties, lands, and mammon, and in achieving goals that will highlight the excellence of our work, that we 'have omitted the weightier matters of the law.' . . . However talented men may be in administrative matters; however eloquent they may be in expressing their views; however learned they may be in the worldly things—they will be denied the sweet whisperings of the Spirit that might have been theirs unless they pay the price of studying, pondering, and praying about the scriptures."[16]

The Prophet Joseph learned by his own experience that those who have the gift of the Holy Ghost will read the scriptures with greater understanding. After he and Oliver Cowdery were baptized, he said, "We were filled with the Holy Ghost, and rejoiced. . . . Our minds being now enlightened, we began to have the scriptures laid open to our understandings, and the true meaning and intention of their more mysterious passages revealed unto us in a manner which we never could attain to previously, nor ever before had thought of" (Joseph Smith–History 1:73–74).

The importance of scripture study can be seen when, almost immediately after the Church was organized, the Lord directed the Prophet Joseph to begin an intense review and translation of the scriptures. Over the next three years Joseph analyzed the entire Bible from Genesis through Revelation. Although his studies were often interrupted by the pressing business of running the Church and by increasing persecution, the Prophet made time to read the scriptures and to ponder intensely and pray about what he was reading. From 1830 to 1833 scripture study engaged most of his time. The result was numerous revelations for him personally, for the Church generally, and for future generations (us). Almost all of the revelations in the Doctrine and Covenants came as a direct result of Joseph Smith's studying the scriptures and pondering.

We can receive answers to highly specific questions when we study the scriptures—not because we can look up questions in the index and find a list of ready references but because reading the scriptures puts our hearts in tune with the Holy Spirit. And the Holy Spirit knows all things, including all the answers to our prayers.

President Ezra Taft Benson promised that those who study the scriptures, particularly the Book of Mormon, will be blessed "with increased discernment to judge between Christ and anti-Christ. . . . with increased power to do good and to resist evil."[17] "There is a power in the book [the Book of Mormon] which will begin to flow into your lives the moment you begin a serious study of [it]."[18]

Elder Bruce R. McConkie echoed that testimony: "People who study the scriptures get a dimension to their life that nobody else gets and that can't be gained in any way except by studying the scriptures. There's an increase in faith and a desire to do what's right and a feeling of inspiration and understanding that comes to people who study the gospel—meaning particularly the Standard Works—and who ponder the principles, that can't come in any other way."[19]

The Prophet Joseph said simply that those who read the scriptures will be able to recognize God's Spirit in their lives: "He that can mark the power of Omnipotence, inscribed upon the heavens, can also see God's own handwriting in the sacred volume: and he who reads it oftenest will like it best, and he who is acquainted with it, will know the hand wherever he can see it."[20]

Elder Spencer W. Kimball testified how his scripture study put him in tune with the Spirit: "I find that when I get casual in my relationships with divinity and when it seems that no divine ear is listening and no divine voice is speaking, that I am far, far away. If I immerse myself in the scriptures the distance narrows and the spirituality returns. I find myself loving more intensely those whom I must love with all my heart and mind and strength, and loving them more, I find it easier to abide their counsel."[21]

Scripture reading is its own reward. "Thy word is a lamp unto my feet, and a light unto my path" (Psalm 119:105). President Brigham Young noted that by studying the scriptures, we "may begin to . . . find out something about God, and begin to learn who he is."[22] Moses and the children of Israel were commanded: "And these words, which I command thee this day, shall be in thine heart: And thou shalt teach them diligently unto thy children, and shalt talk of them when thou sittest in thine house, and when thou walkest by the way, and when thou liest down, and when thou risest up" (Deuteronomy 6:6–7).

Personal righteousness. Someone has said that the best pillow at night is a clear conscience. Living the gospel brings inner peace—peace of mind, peace of soul, peace of conscience. Isaiah said: "And the work of righteousness shall be peace; and the effect of righteousness quietness and assurance for ever. And my people shall dwell in a peaceable habitation, and in sure dwellings, and in quiet resting places" (Isaiah 32:17–18). He also said that in the day when righteousness will cover the earth, the result will be peace: "The whole earth is at rest, and is quiet" (Isaiah 14:7). To whom will revelation be given? The Lord declared, "He that hath clean hands, and a pure heart" (Psalm

24:4). Those who stay close to the Spirit through obedience will be guided in wisdom's paths and be blessed, prospered, and preserved (Mosiah 2:36). Obedience to the principles of the restored gospel brings temporal as well as spiritual blessings.

President Brigham Young taught that sincere repentance and a quick turning of our hearts back to God will keep us close to the Spirit: "I do not recollect that I have seen five minutes since I was baptized that I have not been ready to preach a funeral sermon, lay hands on the sick, or to pray in private or in public. I will tell you the secret of this. In all your business transactions, words, and communications, if you commit an overt act, repent of that immediately, and call upon God to deliver you from evil and give you the light of His spirit. Never do a thing that your conscience, and the light within you, tell you is wrong. Never do a wrong, but do all the good you possibly can. Never do a thing to mar the peaceable influence of the Holy Spirit in you; then whatever you are engaged in—whether in business, in the dance, or in the pulpit—you are ready to officiate at any time in any of the ordinances of the House of God. If I commit an overt act, the Lord knows the integrity of my heart, and through sincere repentance, He forgives me."[23]

Avoiding contention. Anger disrupts inner quiet and chases peace away. "I will be quiet, and will be no more angry" (Ezekiel 16:42). The Prophet Joseph taught, "When a man is borne down with trouble, when he is perplexed with care and difficulty, if he can meet a smile instead of an argument or a murmur—if he can meet with mildness, it will calm down his soul and soothe his feelings; when the mind is going to despair, it needs a solace of affection and kindness."[24]

Reverence. The lack of reverence in our meetings could be costing us the spirit of revelation. If quiet and reverent souls are more able to be in tune with the whisperings of the still small voice, then loud, irreverent souls must be spiritually deaf. At the dedication of the Washington D.C. Temple, President Spencer W. Kimball shared a poem about reverence. Part of it reads:

Enter this door as if the floor within were gold;
And every wall of jewels all of wealth untold;

As if a choir in robes of fire were singing here;
Nor shout nor rush but hush . . . for God is here.[25]

No fear of silence. Often teachers are uncomfortable with even a few seconds of silence in a classroom. But inspired silence allows the Holy Ghost to work on people's hearts. Excellent teachers learn not to fear silence after they have asked a question but to allow for what Elder Neal A. Maxwell has called "moments of deliberate pause."[26] Some of the best teaching takes place when nothing is being said and the Spirit is doing the teaching. Elder Maxwell has also counseled, "Be still, and let that stillness operate on those special occasions when the Spirit informs, inspires, or may call something to someone's remembrance."[27]

An Hour of Peace

We sing: "There is an hour of peace and rest, unmarred by earthly care"[28]—or at least there should be. Daily prayer, meditating on the scriptures, living the gospel, avoiding contention, creating reverence in meetings, and wise use of silence can help us find that hour of "peace and rest" from the world so we can commune with God. Meditative time gives God the opportunity to tell us what he wants us to do. That is when the power of heaven can come to us and we can have the blessing given to King Jehoshaphat: "The realm of Jehoshaphat was quiet: for his God gave him rest round about" (2 Chronicles 20:30). We can experience what the psalmist described: "Then are they glad because they be quiet; so he bringeth them unto their desired haven" (Psalm 107:30).

Notes

1. Woodruff, *Discourses of Wilford Woodruff*, 288–89.
2. Packer, *Ensign*, May 2000, 8.
3. Smith, *Teachings*, 137.

4. Maxwell, *Ensign*, May 1994, 90.
5. Smith, *History of the Church*, 2:170.
6. Smith, *History of the Church*, 1:271.
7. Joseph Smith to Emma Smith, as cited in Berrett, "Letter from the Pen of Joseph Smith," 518, 520; spelling, punctuation, and syntax standardized.
8. Smith, *Times and Seasons* 3 (15 June 1842): 825.
9. McKay, *Man May Know for Himself*, 46–47.
10. McKay, "Prayer," in address to seminary and institute teachers, 6 July 1956, as cited in Dahl and Tate, *Lectures on Faith in Historical Perspective*, 274.
11. Roberts, *Comprehensive History of the Church*, 1:131.
12. Pratt, *Key to the Science of Theology*, 120–21.
13. Smith, *Teachings*, 150.
14. Faust, *To Reach Even unto You*, 14.
15. Asay, *Ensign*, November 1978, 53–54.
16. Bruce R. McConkie, Regional Representatives' Seminar, 2 April 1982, 1–2, as cited in Benson, *Ensign*, May 1986, 81.
17. Benson, Conference Report, April 1986, 78.
18. Benson, Conference Report, October 1986, 8.
19. Croft, "Spare Time's Rare to Apostle," 4.
20. Smith, *Teachings*, 56.
21. Kimball, *Teachings of Spencer W. Kimball*, 135.
22. Young, *Journal of Discourses*, 7:333.
23. Young, *Journal of Discourses*, 12:103.
24. Smith, *Teachings*, 228.
25. "Words of Life," 45, as cited in Kimball, "The Things of Eternity—Stand We in Jeopardy?" 7.
26. Maxwell, "Teaching by the Spirit," 4.
27. Maxwell, "Teaching by the Spirit," 5.
28. *Hymns*, no. 144.

Chapter 8

Spiritual Gifts

It is not appropriate to seek a position in the Church, but it is entirely appropriate to seek the gifts of the Spirit to bless us in our individual callings. We do not talk much about spiritual gifts, yet "we believe in the gift of tongues, prophecy, revelation, visions, healing, interpretation of tongues, and so forth" (Article of Faith 7). These and other gifts of the Spirit will bless our lives and help our families.

Covenant Gifts

Although many people receive spiritual gifts, unique gifts are reserved for those who have received the gift of the Holy Ghost. The Prophet Joseph taught: "There are certain key words and signs belonging to the Priesthood which must be observed in order to obtain the blessing [of certain spiritual gifts]. The sign of Peter was to repent and be baptized for the remission of sins, with the promise of the gift of the Holy Ghost; and in no other way is the gift of the Holy Ghost obtained. . . . Cornelius received the Holy Ghost before he was baptized, which was the convincing power of God unto him of the truth of the Gospel, but he could not receive the gift of the Holy Ghost until after he was baptized. . . . Until he obeyed these ordinances and received the gift of the Holy Ghost, by the laying on of hands, according to the order of God, he could not have healed the sick or commanded an evil spirit to come out of a man, and it obey him."[1]

So, although everyone in the world can receive flashes of inspiration from the light of Christ or witnesses from the Holy Ghost, certain gifts of the Spirit are reserved for those who receive the gift of the Holy Ghost. The purpose of these gifts is to anchor them in their faith. "Faith cometh not by signs, but signs [gifts of the Spirit] follow those that believe" (D&C 63:9).

The Earnest of Our Inheritance

Spiritual gifts, including miracles and blessings, are given to the faithful as a witness from God that he is keeping his end of the covenant they made in the waters of baptism. The gifts of the Spirit are evidence that God will keep his covenant to one day give all the blessings he has promised. They are collateral from God, "the earnest of our inheritance," or the "down payment" on the blessings we will later receive in even larger measure (Ephesians 1:14). Those who are baptized, exercise faith in God, and keep their covenants have a lively hope, or expectation, of eternal life (Ether 12:4). When spiritual gifts are manifest in their lives, they may know that God's Spirit is with them and that the covenant they made at baptism is in force.

Dr. Stephen E. Robinson explained that the gifts of the Spirit are an indication that our baptismal covenant is being honored: "If we experience the gifts of the Spirit or the influence of the Holy Ghost, we can know that we are in the covenant relationship, for the gifts and companionship of the Holy Ghost are given to none else. . . .

"Do you feel the influence of the Holy Ghost in your life? Do you enjoy the gifts of the Spirit? Then you can *know* that God accepts your faith, repentance, and baptism. . . . This is perhaps one reason why the Holy Ghost is called the Comforter, because if we enjoy that gift, we can know that our efforts are acceptable—for now—and that we are justified before God by our faith in Christ. And that is comfort indeed."[2]

Absence of these gifts is evidence that the power of the Holy Ghost is not functioning in society (Mormon 1:14; Moroni 7:35–37). The testimony of the Restoration is that revelation and the use of these gifts continues today. Elder Boyd K. Packer testified, "The promptings of the Spirit, the dreams, and the visions and the visitations, and the ministering of angels all are with us now."[3]

Gifts for All Members

In a revelation to the Church, the Lord said, "Ye are commanded in all things to ask of God, who giveth liberally . . . considering the end of your salvation. . . . Wherefore . . . seek ye earnestly the best gifts, always remembering for what they are given; For verily I say unto you, they are given for the benefit of those who love me . . . that all may be benefited that seek or that ask of me" (D&C 46:7–9).

The phrase "best gifts" implies that some gifts are of more value and importance in helping us obtain eternal life. These good gifts come from God and are meant to be enjoyed: "Every good gift and every perfect gift is from above, and cometh down from the Father of lights" (James 1:17). The baptism of fire—the reception of the Holy Ghost—puts us in possession of spiritual gifts. They are generously distributed among the members "as the Lord sees good to bestow. Yet more than one gift may be received by any person who diligently seeks for these things."[4]

The gifts flowing from the Spirit help us live more spiritually and, when exercised appropriately, enable us to be of greater service to others. The wonderful thing about these spiritual gifts is that every Church member has at least one. No one can claim to have no talents, no gifts. "All have not every gift given unto them; for there are many gifts, [but] to every man is given a gift by the Spirit of God" (D&C 46:11). "When, in disgust or discouragement," Elder Marvin J. Ashton noted, "we allow ourselves to reach depressive levels of despair because of our demeaning self-appraisal, it is a sad day for us and a sad day in the eyes of God. For us to conclude that we have no gifts when we judge ourselves by stature, intelligence, grade-point average, wealth, power, position, or external appearance is not only unfair but unreasonable."[5]

The word *gift* is noteworthy. These spiritual manifestations are *gifts*. They are given by the Holy Ghost to bless our lives. True, they can be developed and increased, but they are bestowed by a loving Father in Heaven upon his children.

These spiritual gifts are given by the Lord to worthy individuals for their blessing and for the edifying of the Church. "Suffice it to say," Elder Bruce R. McConkie explained, "that true greatness, from an eternal standpoint, is measured not in worldly station nor in ecclesiastical office, but in the possession of the gifts of the Spirit and in the enjoyment of the things of God."[6]

Whenever the influence of the Holy Ghost abides with an individual, it will be that person's privilege to experience the gifts of the Spirit. As Elder Orson Pratt observed, "Whenever the Holy Ghost takes up its residence in a person, it not only cleanses, sanctifies, and purifies him, in proportion as he yields himself to its influence, but also imparts to him some gift, intended for the benefit of himself and others. No one who has been born of the Spirit, and who remains sufficiently faithful, is left destitute of a spiritual gift."[7] The Prophet Joseph Smith taught that "no man can receive the Holy Ghost without receiving revelations. The Holy Ghost is a revelator."[8] Among the greatest personal revelations we can receive from the Holy Ghost are the gifts of the Spirit.

Through the Prophet Joseph Smith the Lord revealed that the gifts of the Spirit are given to those "who love me and keep all my commandments, *and him that seeketh so to do*" (D&C 46:9; emphasis added). The gifts of the Spirit are given to those who are trying their best to become perfected. They are given to help us do that which the Holy Spirit testifies we should be doing "in all holiness of heart, walking uprightly before [God], . . . with prayer and thanksgiving, . . . that [we] may not be deceived" (D&C 46:7–8). They are given to strengthen us spiritually and to help us avoid being "seduced by evil spirits, or doctrines of devils, or the commandments of men" (D&C 46:7). "Wherefore," the Lord declared, " . . . that ye may not be deceived, seek ye earnestly the best gifts, always remembering for what they are given" (D&C 46:8).

The Prophet Joseph explained that in order to bless us, the gifts of the Spirit must be exercised: "The greatest, the best, and the most useful gifts would be known nothing about by an observer."[9] We need to be participators with the gifts of the Spirit rather than spectators.

Recognizing Our Gifts

There are many ways to know or recognize the gifts of the Spirit in our own lives: carefully rereading our patriarchal blessing; paying close attention to experiences when we feel the Spirit; listening thoughtfully to the comments of those who know us best; pondering priesthood blessings; remembering the promises made to us when we are set apart for Church callings; and most importantly, counseling with the Lord in prayer. The Lord also indicated that the presiding officers of his Church have the gift to discern all spiritual gifts (D&C 46:27, 29), meaning they can discern the authenticity of the spiritual gifts manifest in a person's life.

Many times callings are extended to help us nurture and exercise spiritual gifts we may not even know we have. It takes a lot of prayer and practice to develop spiritual gifts. The Prophet Joseph said that "time and circumstances" are required to develop and "to call these gifts into operation."[10] Accepting and fulfilling Church callings helps provide us with the "time and circumstances" to develop spiritual gifts.

What Are the Gifts of the Spirit?

The scriptures describe numerous gifts of the Spirit, which are as varied and individual as we ourselves are. Not all of them are "visible to the natural vision, or understanding of man; indeed very few of them are," the Prophet Joseph said.[11] But the scriptures describe many of the gifts we can receive.

From Exodus 31:1–6 we learn of the following gifts of the Spirit:

Wisdom
Understanding
Knowledge
All manner of workmanship
Ability to devise cunning works
Ability to work in gold, silver, brass
Ability to cut and set precious stones
Ability to carve timber
Wisdom to make all that God commands

From Doctrine and Covenants 136:28 we learn of these spiritual gifts:
Praising the Lord with music
Dancing unto the Lord
Singing unto the Lord
Offering prayers to the Lord in thanksgiving

From Doctrine and Covenants 46:13–25 we learn of these gifts:
Knowing that Jesus Christ is the Son of God
Believing on the words (testimonies) of those who know that Jesus is the Christ
Knowing differences of administration, or how to administer the kingdom of God
Knowing diversities of operations, to discern whether "operations" or trends in society are of God
Possessing wisdom
Having knowledge and understanding how to teach it to others
Having faith to be healed
Having faith to heal
Understanding the working of miracles
Prophesying
Discerning spirits
Speaking in tongues
Interpreting tongues

The prophet Moroni listed the following gifts of the Spirit in Moroni 10:9–16:

Teaching the word of wisdom
Teaching the word of knowledge
Exercising exceeding great faith
Working mighty miracles
Prophesying concerning all things
Beholding angels and ministering spirits
Speaking in tongues
Interpreting languages and diverse kinds of tongues

The apostle Paul in 1 Corinthians 12:5–10 described these spiritual gifts:

Differences of administration
Diversities of operations
Word of wisdom
Word of knowledge
Faith
Healing
Working miracles
Prophecy
Discerning spirits
Speaking in tongues
Interpreting tongues

In 2 Peter 1:5–8, the prophet Peter described some of the gifts we need to progress and lay hold on eternal life. He promised that "if these things be in you, and abound, they make you that ye shall neither be barren nor unfruitful in the knowledge of our Lord Jesus Christ" (2 Peter 1:8):

Diligence
Faith
Virtue
Knowledge
Temperance (self-control)
Patience
Godliness (Godlike nature)
Brotherly kindness
Charity

Besides these gifts, many other spiritual gifts are illustrated throughout the scriptures, including the following:

- Dreams (Daniel 2; 1 Nephi 2:2)
- Faith to speak directly to the elements and have them obey (Jacob 4:6)
- The ability for seers to see things that otherwise could not be known (Mosiah 8:16–17)
- The ability to be filled with the grace of God (Mosiah 18:16; 27:5; Moroni 10:32–33)
- The ability to converse with angels (Alma 9:21)
- The ability to speak as angels speak (2 Nephi 32:2–3)
- The ability to speak, teach, or preach by the Spirit (D&C 100:5–8)
- The ability to conduct meetings with the influence of the Spirit (Moroni 6:9)
- The ability to write by the power of the Holy Ghost (Moses 6:5)
- The ability to translate languages (Alma 9:21)
- The power to heal (3 Nephi 29:6)
- The power to cast out devils (Mormon 9:24)
- Protection while on the Lord's errand (Mormon 9:24)
- The power to lay hands on the sick and bless them (Mormon 9:24)
- The power to raise the dead to life (D&C 124:100)
- The ability to see God (D&C 93:1; 67:10)
- The promise of eternal life (D&C 14:7; Mosiah 26:20)

Other gifts relate to our personal attributes and demeanor. They include the following:

- Christ's image (his Spirit) engraven on our countenances (Alma 5:19)
- A knowledge from the Spirit that we have been forgiven of sin (Mosiah 4:3; Enos 1:5–6)
- A confirmation that decisions we make are correct (D&C 9:8–9)
- An enlightened mind (D&C 11:13)

The ability to persuade (D&C 121:41)
Long-suffering (D&C 121:41)
Gentleness (D&C 121:41)
Meekness (D&C 121:41)
Love unfeigned (D&C 121:41)
Kindness (D&C 121:42)
Pure knowledge (D&C 121:42)
Virtue (D&C 121:45)

Some gifts are meant to help us know the mind and will of God:

Understand priesthood and experience its powers (D&C 121:45)
Have the Holy Ghost as a constant companion throughout mortality (D&C 121:46)
Ask all things in Jesus' name and have them given unto you (Moses 6:52)
Perceive the thoughts and feelings of others (Alma 40:1)
Sense whether a decision is right or wrong (D&C 9:7–9)
Recognize promptings (D&C 128:1)
Receive warnings (Alma 23:1)
Receive visions (1 Nephi 8)
Experience visitations (Alma 13:24; 19:34; 32:23)
Minister (Isaiah 61:1–3)
Administer (D&C 46:15)
Recognize God's hand in events that are more than mere coincidence (D&C 111)

Elder Marvin J. Ashton of the Twelve identified what he termed "less conspicious" gifts of the Spirit. He named sixteen of them,[12] including the following:

Asking
Listening
Hearing and using a still, small voice
Being able to weep
Avoiding contention
Being agreeable
Avoiding vain repetition

Seeking that which is righteous
Refraining from passing judgment
Looking to God for guidance
Being a disciple
Caring for others
Being able to ponder
Offering prayer
Bearing a mighty testimony
Receiving the Holy Ghost

As you read over these many gifts of the Spirit, did you see some that would bless your life? Did you notice any that could help your family? Were there gifts that would help you in your Church calling? These gifts are generously offered by our Heavenly Father to bless us. We often live beneath our privileges, but we can have so much more than we do, if we will try. President George Q. Cannon once said:

"How many of you are seeking for these gifts that God has promised to bestow? How many of you, when you bow before your Heavenly Father in your family circle or in your secret places, contend for these gifts to be bestowed upon you? How many of you ask the Father in the name of Jesus to manifest Himself to you through these powers and these gifts? Or do you go along day by day like a door turning on its hinges, without having any feeling upon the subject, without exercising any faith whatever, content to be baptized and be members of the Church and to rest there, thinking that your salvation is secure because you have done this? . . .

"If any of us are imperfect, it is our duty to pray for the gift that will make us perfect. Have I imperfections? I am full of them. What is my duty? To pray to God to give me the gifts that will correct these imperfections. If I am an angry man, it is my duty to pray for charity, which suffereth long and is kind. Am I an envious man? It is my duty to pray to seek for charity, which envieth not. So with all the gifts of the Gospel. They are intended for this purpose. No man ought to say, 'Oh, I cannot help this; it is my nature.' He is not justified in it, for the reason that God has promised to give strength to correct these things and to give gifts that will eradicate them. If a man lacks wisdom, it is his duty to ask God for wisdom. The same with everything else. That is the design of God concerning His children. He wants His Saints to be perfected in the truth. For this purpose He gives these gifts, and bestows them upon those who seek after them, in order that they may be a perfect people upon the face of the earth, notwithstanding their many weaknesses, because God has promised to give the gifts that are necessary for their perfection."[13]

Obtaining the Gifts

If these spiritual gifts are available to us, how then can we obtain them? "There are certain qualifications, or personal preparations, indispensably necessary," Elder Parley P. Pratt explained, "without which no person can be a proper candidate for blessings so divine."[14] To prepare ourselves for the blessings of the Spirit, we must be born again, or changed spiritually. "Being born again," the Prophet Joseph Smith taught, "comes by the Spirit of God through ordinances."[15] To receive the glorious gifts of the Spirit, then, requires that a person exercise faith in Christ, determine to keep the commandments, be baptized, and receive the gift of the Holy Ghost by authorized priesthood holders."

Elder Parley P. Pratt described the effect receiving these ordinances has on a faithful individual:

"The baptism of the water and of the Spirit is called a new birth, and it is in reality a repetition of the natural birth, or entrance into the elements of a new existence . . .

"[This ordinance was] instituted from before the foundation of the world as a pattern of the birth, death, resurrection, and new life of man.

"[The candidate's] mind is quickened, his intellectual faculties are aroused to intense activity. He is, as it were, illuminated. He learns more of divine truth in a few days than he could have learned in a lifetime in the best merely human institutions in the world.

"His affections are also purified, exalted, and increased in proportion. He loves his Heavenly Father and Jesus Christ with a perfect love.

He also loves the members of the Church, or the body of Christ, as he loves his own soul; while his bosom swells with the tenderest sympathies and emotions of good will and benevolence for all mankind. He would make any sacrifice that might be expedient to do good. He would lay down his life most cheerfully, without one moment's hesitation or regret, if required of him by the cause of truth. He also feels the spirit of prayer and watchfulness continually, and pours out his soul in the same, and finds he is answered in all things that are expedient. He is now in a fit capacity to exercise some one or more of the spiritual gifts."[16]

The influence of the Spirit can be immediately felt by such individuals. Note how soon after their baptisms the Prophet Joseph Smith and Oliver Cowdery began to experience the gifts of the Spirit: "Immediately on our coming up out of the water after we had been baptized, we experienced great and glorious blessings from our Heavenly Father. No sooner had I baptized Oliver Cowdery, than the Holy Ghost fell upon him, and he stood up and prophesied many things which should shortly come to pass. And again, so soon as I had been baptized by him, I also had the spirit of prophecy, when, standing up, I prophesied concerning the rise of this Church, and many other things connected with the Church, and this generation of the children of men. We were filled with the Holy Ghost, and rejoiced in the God of our salvation. Our minds being now enlightened, we began to have the scriptures laid open to our understandings, and the true meaning and intention of their more mysterious passages revealed unto us in a manner which we never could attain to previously, nor ever before had thought of" (Joseph Smith–History 1:73–74).

After receiving the first principles and ordinances of the gospel, Church members are prepared to seek after spiritual gifts. Although spiritual gifts may be given to us, they require some effort to use appropriately. Elder Dallin H. Oaks reminded us that these gifts do not come "visibly, automatically and immediately to all who have received the gift of the Holy Ghost."[17]

The spiritual gifts are given by the Holy Ghost and are available to all. Individuals may ask for any of the gifts and receive them, but they have to be exercised according to God's will: "The gifts of God are all useful in their place, but when they are applied to that which God does not intend, they prove an injury, a snare and a curse instead of a blessing."[18] It is not enough to say, "If you just had enough faith, you could have a particular spiritual gift." There must also be great humility before God. We must ask, Is the exercise of this gift in accordance with his will? Is it his will that this particular gift be exercised at this particular time? If it is, and we move forward in faith, his will is being done.

In a revelation to the Prophet Joseph Smith recorded in Doctrine and Covenants 46, the Lord described four things we can do to exercise the gifts of the Spirit properly:

First, we must be humble enough to recognize we need God's help and to ask him for the blessing: "He that asketh in the Spirit asketh according to the will of God; wherefore it is done even as he asketh" (D&C 46:30).

Second, as in all eternal blessings, we ask in the name of our Savior, recognizing his power and authority in our lives: "I say unto you, all things must be done in the name of Christ, whatsoever you do in the Spirit" (D&C 46:31).

Third, we must show all the gratitude our "whole soul has power to possess" (Mosiah 2:20) when God gives us any blessing: "Ye must give thanks unto God in the Spirit for whatsoever blessing ye are blessed with" (D&C 46:32). "What doth it profit a man if a gift is bestowed upon him," the Savior asked, "and he receive not the gift? Behold, he rejoices not in that which is given unto him, neither rejoices in him who is the giver of the gift" (D&C 88:33).

Fourth, we "must practise virtue and holiness before [God] continually" (D&C 46:33).

The Prophet Joseph was privileged to exercise the gifts of the Spirit. When early members of the Church followed his counsel and teachings, they also received spiritual blessings. At the dedication of the Kirtland Temple and for several weeks afterward, the outpouring of the Spirit upon many of the Latter-day Saints who were there has been likened unto the day of Pentecost in the meridian of time, when the Saints were "all filled with the Holy Ghost" (Acts 2:4). Elder Orson Pratt said of experiences in Kirtland, "God was there, his angels were there, the Holy Ghost was in the midst of the people, the visions of the

Almighty were opened to the minds of the servants of the Living God. . . . [The Latter-day Saints] were filled from the crown of their heads to the soles of their feet with the power and inspiration of the Holy Ghost. . . . In that Temple, . . . the people were blessed as they never had been blessed for generations and generations."[19]

All the gifts of the Spirit enjoyed by the Church in the days of Jesus Christ are now being enjoyed in the latter-day Church. Writing to the Saints living in the latter days, the prophet Moroni pleaded with us to "lay hold upon every good gift" (Moroni 10:30). The gifts are available to all, men and women alike. They come in an ordered way and are given liberally among the Saints as God sees fit. Not all have the same gift, not all prophesy, not all speak foreign languages fluently, not all work miracles, but all who are worthy receive the gift of the Holy Ghost. And that marvelous gift provides access to all the other gifts of God.

Notes

1. Smith, *Teachings*, 199.
2. Robinson, *Believing Christ*, 94–95.
3. Packer, *Ensign*, November 1989, 16.
4. Smith, *Church History and Modern Revelation*, 1:201.
5. Ashton, *Ensign*, November 1987, 20.
6. McConkie, *Promised Messiah*, 574–75.
7. Pratt, *Masterful Discourses*, 570.
8. Smith, *Teachings*, 328.
9. Smith, *Teachings*, 246.
10. Smith, *Teachings*, 246.
11. Smith, *Teachings*, 244.
12. Ashton, *Ensign*, November 1987, 20.
13. Cannon, "Discourse," *Millennial Star* 56 (23 April 1894): 260–61; see also Cannon, *Gospel Truth*, 1:154–55.
14. Pratt, *Key to the Science of Theology*, 58.
15. Smith, *Teachings*, 162.
16. Pratt, *Key to the Science of Theology*, 59–60.
17. Oaks, "Spiritual Gifts," 30.
18. Smith, *Teachings*, 248.
19. Pratt, *Journal of Discourses*, 18:132.

CHAPTER 9

Immediate Blessings

The Spirit of the Lord cannot be manipulated or controlled, nor can spiritual things be forced. We feel the gentle breeze and know it is there, but we do not control it. "The wind bloweth where it listeth," the Savior taught Nicodemus, "and thou hearest the sound thereof, but canst not tell whence it cometh, and whither it goeth: so is every one that is born of the Spirit" (John 3:8). Like the gentle breezes around us, we feel the influence of the Spirit in our lives, at times more strongly than at others. The Spirit lifts us to higher levels of living and love, all the while gently blowing the chaff away.

Spiritual experiences are given to us in the Lord's "own time, and in his own way, and according to his own will" (D&C 88:68). He who knows all things knows when all things should occur. But the marvelous thing is that our Heavenly Father desires us to have his Spirit and invites us to seek it. We cannot control the Spirit, but some things we can do are so Christlike, so Godlike in their nature that they immediately strengthen the light within and prepare our hearts to be taught by the Spirit. Certain actions will increase our ability to receive the Spirit as well as to immediately feel the Spirit. These include bearing testimony (D&C 100:5–8), expressing gratitude, and participating in the ordinances of the priesthood. There are also other ways, as the Prophet Joseph taught the Saints, to get and keep the Spirit.

Exercising Faith

Faith in Jesus Christ is the first principle of the restored gospel. It is the first thing we must develop and the final thing we must perfect if we are to enjoy an unending flow of the Spirit of the Lord. Joseph Smith taught that God and Jesus Christ have all power and knowledge because of their perfected faith.[1]

Faith is the first principle of the gospel because it is the prime cause, the motivating force of all things. Everything we do is determined by faith. Farmers plant crops because they have faith the crops will grow. If they didn't believe that, they wouldn't expend the effort to plant. People go to school because they believe the investment in time and money will one day yield a greater harvest. We all invest ourselves in various endeavors and experiences because we have faith we will receive bounteous results. President Harold B. Lee said, "Learning by faith requires the bending of the whole soul through worthy living to become attuned to the Holy Spirit of the Lord."[2]

Faith is a strongly held belief that impels us to action, but faith in Jesus Christ is more than a mere belief, or a wish, or a strong desire. It is more than a positive mental attitude or a hope that a person will have a good day. It is real power. In fact, it is the very power by which God does all things.[3] It is a confidence and trust centered in Jesus Christ that leads a person to salvation. It is an anchor to the soul. "Latter-day Saints also have faith in God the Father, the Holy Ghost, priesthood power, and other important aspects of the restored gospel."[4]

True faith enhances the light within our souls and leads us to know God. True faith, like interest, compounds over time. It "brings miracles, visions, dreams, healings, and all the gifts of God that he gives to his Saints. By faith one obtains a remission of sins and eventually is able to dwell in God's presence. A lack of faith leads one to despair, which comes because of iniquity (Moro. 10:22)."[5]

The light within is a product of our faith in God. "Faith is the assurance of things hoped for, the evidence of things not seen" (JST Hebrews 11:1). In other words, our faith in God and our hope (expectation) of eternal life are confirmed by assurances from God—namely, gifts of the

Spirit. Having the Spirit and spiritual blessings in our life is an assurance or guarantee from God that our faith in his promises to us will be realized (Ephesians 1:14; 2 Corinthians 1:22; 5:5).

There is a direct correlation between the strength of the light within and the strength of our faith in God. Moroni declared: "Men began to exercise faith in Christ; and thus by faith, they did lay hold upon every good thing; . . . men also were saved by faith in his name; and by faith, they become the sons of God. And as surely as Christ liveth he spake these words unto our fathers, saying: Whatsoever thing ye shall ask the Father in my name, which is good, in faith believing that ye shall receive, behold, it shall be done unto you" (Moroni 7:25–26).

How do we gain such great faith? Fortunately, the development of faith is based on fixed principles. Faith does not come to one person and skip others capriciously. We all have the capacity to increase our faith. The apostle Paul declared, "Faith cometh by hearing, and hearing by the word of God" (Romans 10:17). It begins with hearing the word of God as found in the scriptures and in the words of modern prophets. Alma taught, "We will compare the word unto a seed. Now, if ye give place, that a seed [or the word] may be planted in your heart, behold, if it be a true seed, or a good seed, if ye do not cast it out by your unbelief, that ye will resist the Spirit of the Lord, behold, it will begin to swell within your breasts. . . . Now behold, would not this increase your faith? I say unto you, Yea" (Alma 32:28–29).

Planting the words of prophets and scriptures in our hearts will cause our faith to increase until it one day springs up unto everlasting life (Alma 33:23). Certain ideas, when planted in the minds of rational beings, lead them to faith. The Prophet Joseph said, "Let us here observe, that after any portion of the human family are made acquainted with the important fact that there is a God, who has created and does uphold all things, the extent of their knowledge respecting his character and glory will depend upon their diligence and faithfulness in seeking after him, until, like Enoch, the brother of Jared, and Moses, they shall obtain faith in God, and power with him to behold him face to face."[6]

Following Prophets

The Prophet Joseph Smith asked what would motivate individuals to want to see for themselves, to increase their faith in order to have eternal life. He answered, "We have now clearly set forth how it is, and how it was, that God became an object of faith for rational beings; and also, upon what foundation the testimony was based which excited the inquiry and diligent search of the ancient saints to seek after and obtain a knowledge of the glory of God; and we have seen that it was human testimony, and human testimony only, that excited this inquiry, in the first instance, in their minds. It was the credence they gave to the testimony of their fathers, this testimony having aroused their minds to inquire after the knowledge of God; the inquiry frequently terminated, indeed always terminated when rightly pursued, in the most glorious discoveries and eternal certainty."[7]

Hearing the testimony and following the counsel given by living prophets, then, is another way to bring the Spirit into our lives. When God called Enoch to be his prophet, he said, "Behold my Spirit is upon you, wherefore all thy words will I justify; . . . and thou shalt abide in me, and I in you" (Moses 6:34). When a prophet speaks for God, it is as if God himself were speaking (D&C 1:38).

When Enoch was called as a prophet, he was commanded to cover his eyes with clay and then wash them clean. He was promised that afterwards he would "see." It was as if the Lord were saying, "Wash away the things of this world from your life and from your sight, and you will see by the power of the Spirit." Enoch did so and became a seer: "And he beheld the spirits that God had created; and he beheld also things which were not visible to the natural eye [to the natural man]; and from thenceforth came the saying abroad in the land: A seer hath the Lord raised up unto his people" (Moses 6:36).

The spectrum of light and intelligence is very wide. As mortals we can see and comprehend only a limited amount. But seers have a wider view: "A seer is a revelator and a prophet also. . . . A seer can know of things which are past, and also of things which are to come, and by them shall all things be revealed, or, rather, shall secret things be made manifest, and hidden things shall come to light, and things which are not known shall be made known by them, and also things shall be made known by them which otherwise could not be known. . . . Therefore he becometh a great benefit to his fellow beings" (Mosiah 8:16–18). "What great, eternal light and knowledge comes to us," Elder M. Russell Ballard testified, "from the marvelous revelations from God to His faithful prophets."[8]

Joseph Smith was called of God, as are all prophets and seers. Joseph was a prophet, and he is the prophet who stands at the head of this final dispensation of the fulness of times. Joseph said humbly of his own calling: "You don't know me. . . . No man knows my history. I cannot tell it: I shall never undertake it. I don't blame any one for not believing my history. If I had not experienced what I have, I could not have believed it myself. . . . When I am called by the trump of the archangel and weighed in the balance, you will all know me then."[9]

Great spiritual light and protection has been promised to those who follow the counsel of the prophets: "The gates of hell shall not prevail against you, yea, and the Lord God will disperse the powers of darkness from before you, and cause the heavens to shake for your good, and his name's glory" (D&C 21:6).

Where do the words of the living prophets stand with respect to the written scriptures? Both are important, but, as President Ezra Taft Benson said, the words of the living prophet are even more vital than the standard works.[10] President Wilford Woodruff spoke of an incident in which the Prophet Joseph Smith taught the Saints this principle: "Brother Joseph turned to Brother Brigham Young and said, 'Brother Brigham, I want you to take the stand and tell us your views with regard to the written oracles and the written word of God.' Brother Brigham took the stand, and he took the Bible, and laid it down; he took the Book of Mormon, and laid it down; and he took the Book of Doctrine and Covenants, and laid it down before him, and he said: 'There is the written word of God to us, concerning the work of God from the beginning of the world, almost, to our day.'

"'And now,' said he, 'when compared with the living oracles those books are nothing to me; those books do not convey the word of God direct to us now, as do the words of a Prophet or a man bearing the

Holy Priesthood in our day and generation. I would rather have the living oracles than all the writing in the books.' That was the course he pursued. When he was through, Brother Joseph said to the congregation: 'Brother Brigham has told you the word of the Lord, and he has told you the truth.'"[11]

It takes faith to follow the counsel of prophets, but those who do are blessed with even greater faith. Obedience to their counsel brings greater spirituality. In 1836 a School of the Prophets was organized to train missionaries to preach the gospel more effectively. Small groups of missionaries gathered in the temple to hear the words of the Prophet before heading out to their respective fields of labor. Each room in the upper level of the temple was occupied by a different priesthood quorum. The Prophet Joseph gave each group the same instructions about how to proceed and how to pray so that they might enjoy an outpouring of the Spirit. "The quorum of Elders had not observed the order which I had given them," the Prophet recounted. "This caused the Spirit of the Lord to withdraw, . . . and this quorum lost their blessing in a great measure.

"The other quorums were more careful, and . . . enjoyed a great flow of the Holy Spirit. Many arose and spoke, testifying that they were filled with the Holy Ghost, which was like fire in their bones, so that they could not hold their peace, but were constrained to cry hosanna to God and the Lamb, and glory in the highest. . . . This was a time of rejoicing long to be remembered."[12] Those who followed the Prophet's counsel were blessed in great measure; the others were not. Today, we can all hear or read the words of the living prophets, so in a sense, all Church members belong to a "School of the Prophets." What a great privilege! Following the counsel of the living prophet will bring wonderful blessings to our lives and the lives of our families.

Humble and Sincere Prayer

Our Heavenly Father presides over a vast kingdom. He has an innumerable host of children scattered throughout the immensity of space. But his kingdom is unlike any kingdom on earth: he invites every one of his subjects to petition him—daily! He promises that he will hear and answer all petitions that are brought before him in humility and in sincerity. Humble prayer is the door by which we access the light within. "Let him that is ignorant learn wisdom by humbling himself and calling upon the Lord his God, that his eyes may be opened that he may see, and his ears opened that he may hear; for my Spirit is sent forth into the world to enlighten the humble and contrite" (D&C 136:32–33). If there is anything we don't understand, he has invited us to ask him and to let our hearts "be full, drawn out in prayer unto him continually for [our] welfare" (Alma 34:27). Learning to pray cultivates the Holy Spirit within our souls.

It is a great privilege to ask God anytime and anywhere about any subject. We can rest assured that he knows everything about anything we may want to ask about: "O how great the holiness of our God! For he knoweth all things, and there is not anything save he knows it" (2 Nephi 9:20). "He looketh down upon all the children of men; and he knows all the thoughts and intents of the heart"(Alma 18:32). The question naturally arises, If God knows our needs and knows what we are going to pray about, why, then, do we need to pray? The answer is perfectly clear. We pray precisely because God does know all things—and we don't. We pray to put our hearts and minds and souls in tune with the Spirit of God so that we too can know. But we also pray to strengthen our personal relationship with our Heavenly Father. Communication is critically important in relationships.

Joseph Smith taught us how to pray and how to approach God so that our prayers can be answered. He studied the scriptures searching for answers. He listened to the promptings of the Spirit that motivated him to pray. He prayed aloud and his prayers were heard. From that time on he was able to declare, "All is well . . . I have learned for myself" (Joseph Smith–History 1:20).

Our Heavenly Father has invited all of us to approach him in prayer. He promises that he will answer: "Be thou humble; and the Lord thy God shall lead thee by the hand, and give thee answer to thy prayers" (D&C 112:10). There is power in spoken prayers because God can reveal answers to us through the words we are inspired to speak.

Joseph Smith believed in the power of prayer. "It is the privilege," he said, "of the Children of God to come to God and get Revelation."[13] He knew through experience that God was accessible, that prayer unlocks the powers of heaven in our behalf. His prayers were humble and filled with confidence that God would hear and answer. His diary furnishes evidence of his sincere search for personal salvation. He prayed often to be forgiven, for peace of mind, for help in overcoming weakness. His diary entries illustrate his prayerful attitude: "O may God grant that I may be directed in all my thoughts," or "Lord bless my family and preserve them." It is not uncommon to read a letter Joseph wrote and see prayers inserted mid-sentence for the person to whom the letter was being written. Some of his prayers were urgent: "O Lord deliver thy servant out of temptations and fill his heart with wisdom and understanding." Writing about a meeting that had been held, he said, "A great congregation paid good attention. Oh God, seal our testimony to their hearts." On another occasion he prayed for the work to go forward: "Oh God, establish thy word among this people."[14]

The Prophet firmly believed in the power of prayer and on one occasion said, "The best way to obtain truth and wisdom is not to ask it from books, but to go to God in prayer, and obtain divine teaching."[15] But he maintained a balanced approach to learning by the Spirit. He received a revelation reminding us to "seek . . . diligently and teach one another words of wisdom; yea, seek . . . out of the best books words of wisdom; seek learning, even by study and also by faith" (D&C 88:118).

Daniel Tyler attended a meeting in which he heard Joseph pray, and he was moved by how intimately and humbly the Prophet addressed God: "Never until then had I heard a man address his Maker as though He was present listening as a kind father would listen to the sorrows of a dutiful child. Joseph was at that time unlearned, but that prayer, which was to a considerable extent in behalf of those who accused him of having gone astray and fallen into sin, that the Lord would forgive them and open their eyes that they might see aright—that prayer, I say, to my humble mind, partook of the learning and eloquence of heaven. There was no ostentation, no raising of the voice as by enthusiasm, but a plain conversational tone, as a man would address a present friend. It appeared to me as though, in case the vail were taken away, I could see the Lord standing facing His humblest of all servants I had ever seen. . . . It was the crowning . . . of all the prayers I ever heard."[16]

Joseph also trusted in the prayers of others. Once, while being pursued by enemies who were threatening him with violence, the Prophet "was told that quite a number of little children were gathered together praying for his safety. He replied: 'Then I need have no fear; I am safe.'"[17]

Singing Hymns

"The singing of hymns is one of the best ways to put ourselves in tune with the Spirit of the Lord," Elder Dallin H. Oaks testified. "I wonder if we are making enough use of this heaven-sent resource in our meetings, in our classes, and in our homes."[18]

In a revelation given to the Prophet Joseph in July 1830, just three months after the Church was organized, he was instructed to call his wife, Emma, "to make a selection of sacred hymns, as it shall be given thee, which is pleasing unto me, to be had in my church. For my soul delighteth in the song of the heart; yea, the song of the righteous is a prayer unto me, and it shall be answered with a blessing upon their heads" (D&C 25:11–12).

Elder Joseph Young recorded how involved the Prophet Joseph was with music in the Church:

"This subject [music] came under the especial notice of Joseph Smith, the Prophet, who organized the first choir in the church, and who was a constant attendant at their singing schools. He recommended the Saints to cultivate as high a state of perfection in their musical harmonies as the standard of the faith which he had brought was superior to sectarian religion. To obtain this, he gave them to understand that the refinement of singing would depend on the attainment of the Holy Spirit. . . .

"When this subject is studied and sought after by the singers of the Saints, with their whole hearts, their songs and anthems, and their minstrels, will soften into celestial melody, melt the hearts of the Saints and draw them together, as the magnet needle is drawn to the lodestone."[19]

Early on Christmas morning in 1843, the Prophet Joseph was surprised by carolers singing outside his window: "This morning, about one o'clock, I was aroused by an English sister, Lettice Rushton, widow of Richard Rushton, Senior, (who, ten years ago, lost her sight,) accompanied by three of her sons, with their wives, and her two daughters, with their husbands, and several of her neighbors, singing, 'Mortals, awake! with angels join,' &c., which caused a thrill of pleasure to run through my soul. All of my family and boarders arose to hear the serenade, and I felt to thank my Heavenly Father for their visit, and blessed them in the name of the Lord. They also visited my brother Hyrum, who was awakened from his sleep. He arose and went out of doors. He shook hands with and blessed each one of them in the name of the Lord, and said that he thought at first that a cohort of angels had come to visit him, it was such heavenly music to him."[20]

Eunice Billings Snow remembered as a little girl how impressed she was with Joseph Smith's love for music: "I went to school with the Prophet Joseph's children. . . . During the persecution of the Prophet, especially when he was in hiding, he would sometimes be allowed to visit his family for an evening, and would request my father and mother to come to sing for him. They would take me with them, and when Joseph found that I could sing a part alone he requested them to bring me. We would sing his favorite hymns: 'When Joseph His Brethren Beheld,' 'Redeemer of Israel,' 'The Spirit of God,' and several others. He would become so inspired with the spirit of the music that he would clap his hands and shout hosanna to the Lord.

"He would have me sit close to him, and laying his hands on my head would say, 'My little sister, you will be able to sing the songs of Zion as long as you desire.' He also blessed me on different occasions. I was always very much affected by the Spirit which he manifested. At first I did not know what it was, but my mother told me it was the power which Joseph possessed."[21]

Music has always been a source of comfort to the Saints in times of trial. Just before leaving the Last Supper in the Upper Room and going to Gethsemane, the Savior and his apostles sang a hymn

(Matthew 26:30). Similarly, Joseph Smith asked John Taylor to sing "A Poor Wayfaring Man of Grief" shortly before Joseph was martyred. Three years later, Sister Nancy Tracy recalled, music was heard coming from the Nauvoo Temple just hours before her group departed from their beloved city for the last time: "About the last of May, previous to our departure from Nauvoo, I was aroused from my slumbers one night, hearing such heavenly music as I had never heard before. Everything was so still and quiet when it burst upon my ear that I could not imagine where it came from. I got up and looked out of the window. The moon shone bright as I looked over at the [Nauvoo] Temple from whence the sound came. There on the roof of the building heavenly bands of music had congregated and were playing most beautifully. The music was exquisite!"[22]

The trek across the plains was also filled with music. In a revelation given to organize the pioneer companies for their long trek west, they were told, "If thou art merry, praise the Lord with singing, with music, with dancing, and with a prayer of praise and thanksgiving" (D&C 136:28). As they crossed the continent, they played music and danced almost every night.

Beautiful music brings the Spirit of the Lord. Brigham Young said, "Everything that is joyful, beautiful, glorious, comfortable, consoling, lovely, pleasing to the eye, good to the taste, pleasant to the smell, and happifying in every respect is for the Saints. Tight-laced religious professors of the present generation have a horror at the sound of a fiddle. There is no music in hell, for all good music belongs to heaven. Sweet harmonious sounds give exquisite joy to human beings capable of appreciating music. . . . Every sweet musical sound that can be made belongs to the Saints and is for the Saints. Every flower, shrub, and tree to beautify and to gratify the taste and smell, and every sensation that gives to man joy and felicity are for the Saints who receive them from the Most High."[23]

Temple Worship

The temple is the house of the Lord. The Prophet Joseph dedicated the first temple built in this dispensation at Kirtland, Ohio, so that "the

Son of Man might have a place to manifest himself to his people" (D&C 109:5). The temple is a spiritual place where we "receive a fulness of the Holy Ghost . . . and [are] prepared to obtain every needful thing" (D&C 109:15). Elder David B. Haight testified: "The moment we step into the house of the Lord, the atmosphere changes from the worldly to the heavenly, where respite from the normal activities of life is found, and where peace of mind and spirit is received. It is a refuge from the ills of life and a protection from the temptations that are contrary to our spiritual well-being. We are told that 'he who doeth the works of righteousness shall receive his reward, even peace in this world, and eternal life in the world to come.' (D&C 59:23.)"[24]

Information necessary for our exaltation in God's presence is taught in the temple. In fact, Joseph Smith was told, temple ordinances are the "most glorious of all subjects belonging to the everlasting gospel" (D&C 128:17). The Savior promised that the Saints would be "endowed with power from on high" in the temple (D&C 38:32). President Ezra Taft Benson testified that part of that endowment includes personal revelation: "The temple is the house of the Lord. Our attendance there . . . blesses us, for it is a house of revelation."[25] He further testified: "I promise you that, with increased attendance in the temples of our God, you shall receive increased personal revelation to bless your life as you bless those who have died."[26]

President Benson further taught: "In the peace of these lovely temples, sometimes we find solutions to the serious problems of life. Under the influence of the Spirit, sometimes pure knowledge flows to us there. Temples are places of personal revelation. When I have been weighed down by a problem or a difficulty, I have gone to the House of the Lord with a prayer in my heart for answers. These answers have come in clear and unmistakable ways."[27]

The spirit which pervades the temple is but a foretaste of an eternal promise to the faithful, which the Lord revealed to Joseph Smith: "I will come unto you. . . . I will visit you with the joy of my countenance" (D&C 88:52–53). Often the meetings the Prophet held in the temple were blessed with significant spiritual manifestations, including visitations by the Savior himself (D&C 110:1–4). At his appearance in the Kirtland Temple, the Savior promised: "Let the hearts of all my people rejoice. . . . For behold, I have accepted this house, and my name shall be here; and I will manifest myself to my people in mercy in this house. Yea, I will appear unto my servants, and speak unto them with mine own voice, if my people will keep my commandments, and do not pollute this holy house. Yea the hearts of thousands and tens of thousands shall greatly rejoice in consequence of the blessings which shall be poured out" (D&C 110:6–9).

The Saints were driven from Kirtland and eventually to Nauvoo. The Prophet Joseph urged them to move forward and fulfill the Lord's command to construct another temple, in which those blessings could again be realized. Joseph worked alongside others in the quarry chiseling out stone for the temple, but he would not live to see it completed. After his martyrdom, the Saints redoubled their efforts to finish the temple. The temple finally opened in December 1845. The Saints were eager to receive their temple blessings. On January 5, 1846, 144 people received their temple blessings. The next day, 90 people received the ordinances. On January 7, President Brigham Young said, "This morning there was an immense crowd at the reception room, waiting for admission. One hundred and twenty-one persons received the ordinances." Just a few days later he writes: "Such has been the anxiety manifested by the saints to receive the ordinances, and such the anxiety on our part to administer them, that I have given myself up entirely to the work of the Lord in the Temple night and day, not taking more than four hours sleep, upon an average, per day, and going home but once a week. Elder Heber C. Kimball and others of the Twelve Apostles are in constant attendance but in consequence of close application some of them have had to leave the Temple, to rest and recruit their health.'"[28]

Soon persecutions came and the Saints were also driven from Nauvoo. Brigham Young had given word that the time had come for temple work to cease so that the Church could depart into the wilderness. In President Young's history, under the date of Tuesday, 3 February, is the following entry:

"Notwithstanding that I had announced that we would not attend to the administration of the ordinances, the House of the Lord was thronged all day, the anxiety being so great to receive, as if the brethren would have us stay here and continue the endowments until our way would be hedged up, and our enemies would intercept us. But I informed the brethren that this was not wise, and that we should build more Temples, and have further opportunities to receive the blessings of the Lord, as soon as the saints were prepared to receive them. In this Temple we have been abundantly rewarded, if we receive no more. I also informed the brethren that I was going to get my wagons started and be off. I walked some distance from the Temple supposing the crowd would disperse, but on returning I found the house filled to overflowing.

"Looking upon the multitude and knowing their anxiety, as they were thirsting and hungering for the word, we continued at work diligently in the House of the Lord.

"Two hundred and ninety-five persons received ordinances."[29]

The work continued throughout the week, day and night. On Friday, 6 February, 512 more people received temple blessings. On Saturday, 7 February, almost 600 more did also. The temple was then closed for ordinance work and the pioneers began their trek west. The Lord had promised that their temple blessings would sustain them as they headed across the plains (D&C 136:4, 11).

President George Q. Cannon noted how eager the Saints in Joseph Smith's day were to receive their temple blessings: "When the Prophet Joseph first communicated that the Lord had revealed to him the keys of the endowment, I can remember the great desire there was on every hand to understand something about them. When the Prophet would speak about his desire to complete the temple in order that he might impart unto his fellow servants that which God had delivered to him, a thrill went through the congregation and a great desire for this filled their hearts. . . .

"Then, when he did communicate the endowments to a few persons before the temple was completed, the whole people were moved with desire to complete the temple in order that they might receive these great blessings therein. They were valued beyond price. A man that could go in and get his endowments was looked upon as though he had received some extraordinary blessing—something akin to that which the angels received—and it was estimated and valued in that way.

"How is it now? There is a complete indifference, it may be said, in relation to it. Young people go there . . . with no particular desire only to get married, without realizing the character of the obligations that they take upon themselves or the covenants that they make and the promises involved in the taking of these covenants. The result is, hundreds among us go to the house of the Lord and receive these blessings and come away without having any particular impression made upon them.

"I think that this is deplorable. When men have gifts and blessings bestowed upon them and they do not value them, they become a cause of condemnation rather than blessing. It seems to me that there should be exceeding great care taken in this respect."[30]

Immediate Blessings

Sometimes we may feel that having the Spirit in our lives involves a long, drawn-out process. The Prophet Joseph Smith tried to help the Saints see that faith, hearing the word, following the counsel of prophets, humble prayer, the power of righteous music, and temple worship can bring an immediate response from the Spirit. Bearing testimony, expressing gratitude, singing the hymns of the Restoration, hearing the testimony of others, and so forth, bring immediate feelings of humility, repentance, a desire to improve our lives, and a hope and determination to do what is right. As Elder Gene R. Cook has observed, "When that occurs, an individual has truly been taught by the power of the Spirit."[31]

Notes

1. Smith, *Lectures on Faith* 7:2.
2. Lee, Conference Report, April 1971, 94.

3. Smith, *Lectures on Faith* 7:3–4.
4. *Guide to the Scriptures*, 80.
5. *Guide to the Scriptures*, 81.
6. Smith, *Lectures on Faith* 2:55.
7. Smith, *Lectures on Faith* 2:56.
8. Ballard, *Ensign*, May 1998, 33.
9. Smith, *Teachings*, 361–62.
10. Benson, "Fourteen Fundamentals."
11. Woodruff, Conference Report, October 1897, 22–23.
12. Smith, *History of the Church*, 2:392.
13. Ehat and Cook, *Words of Joseph Smith*, 13.
14. Jesse, *Personal Writings of Joseph Smith*, 16–19; spelling and punctuation modernized.
15. Smith, *Teachings*, 191.
16. Tyler, "Recollections of the Prophet Joseph Smith," 127–28.
17. Jane Snyder Richards, *Young Woman's Journal* 16 (December 1905): 550, as cited in Andrus and Andrus, *They Knew the Prophet*, 165–66.
18. Oaks, *Ensign*, November 1994, 10.
19. Young, *History of the Organization of the Seventies*, 15.
20. Smith, *History of the Church*, 6:134.
21. Eunice Billings Snow, *Woman's Exponent* 39 (August 1910): 14, as cited in Andrus and Andrus, *They Knew the Prophet*, 152.
22. Nancy Tracy Autobiography, typescript, 32, in Special Collections, Harold B. Lee Library, Brigham Young University, as cited in *LDS Collector's Library*.
23. Arrington, *Brigham Young*, 289.
24. Haight, *Ensign*, November 1990, 61.
25. Benson, Conference Report, April 1986, 100.
26. Benson, *Ensign*, May 1987, 85.
27. Benson, "What I Hope You Will Teach Your Children," August 1985, 8.
28. Smith, *History of the Church*, 7:567.
29. Smith, *History of the Church*, 7:579.
30. Cannon, *Gospel Truth*, 1:228.
31. "Preparing for Influence of Holy Ghost," 7.

CHAPTER 10

Principles of Personal Revelation

Personal revelation is one of the most important gifts given to mankind. Revelation from heaven changes lives. The revelations given to the Prophet Joseph Smith have had a profound effect on individuals' lives throughout the whole world. His teachings record a strong emphasis on personal revelation. The Book of Mormon and the Doctrine and Covenants contain more verses regarding personal revelation than other books of scripture. Joseph Smith was well acquainted with the principles governing the light within.

Continuing Revelation

It is both reasonable and scriptural to believe in continuing modern revelation. Joseph Smith declared that "Jesus in His teachings says, 'Upon this rock I will build my Church, and the gates of hell shall not prevail against it.' What rock? Revelation."[1]

Joseph noted that continuing revelation is a part of God's plan: "We have what we have, and the Bible contains what it does contain:

but to say that God never said anything more to man than is there recorded, would be saying at once that we have at last received a revelation: . . . because it is nowhere said in that volume by the mouth of God, that He would not, after giving what is there contained, speak again; and if any man has found out for a fact that the Bible contains all that God ever revealed to man he has ascertained it by an immediate revelation, other than has been previously written by the prophets and apostles."[2]

The Order of Revelation

There is an order, or stewardship, for revelation. "I will inform you," the Prophet Joseph taught, "that it is contrary to the economy of God for any member of the Church, or any one, to receive instruction for those in authority, higher than themselves; therefore you will see the impropriety of giving heed to them; but if any person have a vision or a visitation from a heavenly messenger, it must be for his own benefit and instruction; for the fundamental principles, government, and doctrine of the Church are vested in the keys of the kingdom."[3] Revelation for others comes only to those who have been properly called, sustained, and ordained or set apart. "For my house is a house of order, saith the Lord God" (D&C 132:18). Personal revelation is precisely that—personal—and meant only for the recipient. Visions, dreams, or promptings do not of themselves empower anyone to speak for, or to, others. "It shall not be given to any one to go forth to preach my gospel, or to build up my church, except he be ordained by some one who has authority, and it is known to the church that he has authority and has been regularly ordained by the heads of the Church" (D&C 42:11). Each member is privileged to "act in the office in which [he or she is] appointed" (D&C 107:99). But only the president of the Church receives revelation for the Church (D&C 28:1–7).[4] All other leaders and members receive revelation limited to their own stewardships and callings. "Few things disturb the channels of revelation quite so effectively as those who are misled and think themselves to be chosen to instruct others when they are not chosen."[5]

Personal revelation does not empower an individual with authority to preside over others. Elder Dallin H. Oaks, quoting Elder Boyd K. Packer, has stated: "Individuals can receive revelation to guide their own lives. But when one person purports to receive revelation for another person outside his or her own stewardship—such as a Church member who claims to have revelation to guide the entire Church or a person who claims to have revelation to guide another person over whom he or she has no presiding authority according to the order of the Church—you can be sure that such revelations are not from the Lord. 'There are counterfeit signals' (Boyd K. Packer, 'Prayers and Answers,' *Ensign*, November 1979, p. 20). Satan is a great deceiver, and he is the source of some of these spurious revelations. Others are simply imagined. If a revelation is outside the limits of stewardship, you know it is not from the Lord, and you are not bound by it."[6]

Seek Diligently

Those who inquire of God provide him opportunities to give answers. Many of the revelations recorded in the Doctrine and Covenants came as a direct result of Joseph's asking the Lord for enlightenment and answers to questions. To the Saints through the Prophet Joseph the Lord declared, "No good thing will I withhold from them who walk uprightly before me, and do my will in all things—who will listen to my voice and to the voice of my servant whom I have sent; for I delight in those who seek diligently to know my precepts, and abide by the law of my kingdom; for all things shall be made known unto them in mine own due time, and in the end they shall have joy."[7]

The Lord also said to the Prophet Joseph Smith: "If thou shalt ask, thou shalt receive revelation upon revelation, knowledge upon knowledge, that thou mayest know the mysteries and peaceable things—that which bringeth joy, that which bringeth life eternal" (D&C 42:61).

Besides simply asking, the Prophet Joseph also learned, "perspiration must precede inspiration"[8]—personal revelation requires our best mental efforts: "Behold, you have not understood; you have supposed that I would give it unto you, when you took no thought save it was to ask me. But, behold, I say unto you, that you must study it out in your mind; then you must ask me if it be right" (D&C 9:7–8).

Through the Prophet Joseph Smith, the Saints were also promised that if they would "treasure up in your minds continually the words of life, . . . it shall be given you in the very hour that portion that shall be meted unto every man." (D&C 84:85). An old saying states, "You can't get water from an empty well." The more we "treasure" (appreciate, care for, store away) the words of the Lord, the more the Holy Ghost will have to draw from. It is true that the Holy Ghost can "pour" knowledge over us that distills "upon thy soul as the dews from heaven" (D&C 121:45), but two important roles of the Spirit are to "teach you all things, and bring all things to your remembrance, whatsoever I have said unto you" (John 14:26). The more we prepare our minds, the more the Holy Ghost will have to work with. That is why the Lord said to Hyrum Smith, who wanted to serve a mission in 1829, before the Church had been established and before the Book of Mormon had been published, "Wait a little longer, until you shall have my word, my rock, my church, and my gospel, that you may know of a surety my doctrine. . . . Seek not to declare my word, but first seek to obtain my word, and then shall your tongue be loosed; then, if you desire, you shall have my Spirit and my word, yea, the power of God unto the convincing of men. . . . Therefore, treasure up in your heart until the time which is in my wisdom that you shall go forth" (D&C 11:16, 21, 26).

All Can Receive Personal Revelation

Joseph Smith taught authoritatively that men and women have equal status before the Lord. He taught that God honors his daughters just as he does his sons: "For [God] . . . inviteth them all to come unto him and partake of his goodness; and he denieth none that come unto him, black and white, bond and free, male and female; and he remembereth the heathen; and all are alike unto God, both Jew and Gentile" (2 Nephi 26:33). Such language was simply revolutionary and forward-thinking in 1830 when the first edition of the Book of Mormon rolled off the press.

Many passages in Joseph Smith's history record instances in which both men and women received revelations, spoke in tongues, prophesied, had dreams, and exercised other gifts of the Spirit. The Lord has promised he would give "light [to] men, women, and children" (Ether 6:3).

Not All Receive the Same Degree of Revelation

Revelation is a gift from God. Everyone does not have the same gift, or the same gift in the same degree. For example, we may not have the gift of revelation, but that does not mean we cannot receive revelation. We can "believe on the words of others," or receive inspiration through others, until we receive our own witness. In Doctrine and Covenants we learn that "To some is given by the Holy Ghost to know that Jesus Christ is the Son of God, and that he was crucified for the sins of the world. To others it is given to believe on their words, that they also might have eternal life if they continue faithful" (D&C 46:13–14).

Common Consent

The law of common consent was revealed by the Lord so that the Saints could hear Church leaders' decisions and be invited to sustain those decisions (D&C 26:1–2; 28:12–13; 42:11). The law of common consent enables Church members to come to a consensus. There is great safety in staying with the majority in the Church. Most Church members followed Brigham Young to the Rocky Mountains. Only small groups of individuals chose to remain behind. Knowing that some leaders in his day would apostatize from the Church, the Prophet Joseph gave this counsel:

"I will give you a key that will never rust, if you will stay with the majority of the Twelve Apostles . . . you will never be led astray."[9]

Discerning Truth

Although he will not reveal all things to us now, God has promised that the Holy Ghost will help us discern all truth (John 16:12–4). When Joseph Smith was working on his translation of the Bible, he asked the Lord what to do with the Apocrypha, which are uncanonized writings from the period between the Old and New Testaments. The Savior replied: "Verily, thus saith the Lord unto you concerning the Apocrypha—There are many things contained therein that are true, and it is mostly translated correctly; There are many things contained therein that are not true, which are interpolations by the hands of men. Verily, I say unto you, that it is not needful that the Apocrypha should be translated. Therefore, whoso readeth it, let him understand, for the Spirit manifesteth truth; And whoso is enlightened by the Spirit shall obtain benefit therefrom; And whoso receiveth not by the Spirit, cannot be benefited" (D&C 91:1–6).

The same could be said of any number of other books that line bookstore walls. The closer to the Spirit we are in our personal lives, the greater the benefit we can receive as we read. The Lord does not need to send revelation about every single book that is published or every worldly philosophy that is promoted, for "some are of men, and others of devils" (D&C 46:7). The Holy Ghost will help us discern between truth, fiction, and spiritual fraud whether in college texts, business books, works of fiction, movies, or works of self-help, pop-psychologists and self-professed religionists.

Inspiration in Our Callings

"Now, as you have asked, behold, I say unto you, keep my commandments, and seek to bring forth and establish the cause of Zion;

seek not for riches but for wisdom, and behold, the mysteries of God shall be unfolded unto you" (D&C 6:6–7). Often the "mysteries" we seek answers for are not mysterious teachings but such things as "how can I succeed in my calling?" or "how can I touch the lives of those I'm trying to serve?" or "what can I do to help myself and others lay hold on eternal life?" Those who seek to fulfill the callings they hold have been promised revelation: "Blessed are they who shall seek to bring forth my Zion at that day, for they shall have the gift and the power of the Holy Ghost; and if they endure unto the end they shall be lifted up at the last day, and shall be saved in the everlasting kingdom of the Lamb; and whoso shall publish peace, yea, tidings of great joy, how beautiful upon the mountains shall they be" (1 Nephi 13:37).

Having the Spirit in our lives makes our approach to teaching a positive one. We teach others with more hope and love because love is a gift of the Spirit (Moroni 8:26; Ether 12:4). There is power in this kind of teaching—the power to change lives. Elder Gordon B. Hinckley said: "The forces against which we labor are tremendous. We need more than our own strength to cope with them. To all who hold positions of leadership, to the vast corps of teachers and missionaries, to heads of families, I should like to make a plea: In all you do, feed the spirit—nourish the soul. . . . I am satisfied that the world is starved for spiritual food."[10]

Treat Revelation with Care

Personal revelations from God through the Holy Ghost need to be treated with the utmost respect. "Blessed art thou because of thy gift," the Lord told Joseph Smith. "Remember it is sacred and cometh from above" (D&C 6:10). The Lord reminded all of us how precious these gifts of revelation are: "Remember that that which cometh from above is sacred, and must be spoken with care, and by constraint of the Spirit; and in this there is no condemnation, and ye receive the Spirit through prayer; wherefore, without this there remaineth condemnation" (D&C 63:64). Unless we are inspired by the Spirit to do so, sharing personal revelations in unguarded ways violates a sacred trust. Openly sharing sacred personal experiences may draw attention to oneself rather than to the Savior, who is the source of revelation: "Behold I am the light which ye shall hold up" (3 Nephi 18:24).

Generally, a spiritually sound approach to teaching is to find a scripture that illustrates the principle, teach that scripture, and then bear witness that it is true. In this manner, the scriptures become the source for the doctrine, and the Spirit will bear witness of the teacher's testimony.

The Prophet Joseph described how important it is to be trustworthy regarding spiritual communications: "The reason we do not have the secrets of the Lord revealed unto us, is because we do not keep them but reveal them; we do not keep our own secrets, but reveal our difficulties to the world, even to our enemies, then how would we keep the secrets of the Lord? I can keep a secret till Doomsday."[11]

Open discussion before the world of sacred communications will cause the channels of revelation to close. The Prophet Joseph said, "I know much that I do not tell."[12] Joseph was one whom the Lord could trust. Elder Boyd K. Packer offered this caution: "I have learned that strong, impressive spiritual experiences do not come to us very frequently. . . . I have come to believe also that it is not wise to continually talk of unusual spiritual experiences. They are to be guarded with care and shared only when the Spirit itself prompts you to use them to the blessing of others."[13]

Brigham Young counseled that if we want more revelation, we need to prove we can be trusted with it: "You often hear people desiring more of the knowledge of God, more of the wisdom of God, more of the power of God. They want more revelation, to know more about the kingdom of heaven, in heaven and on the earth, and they wish to learn and increase. There is one principle that I wish the people would understand and lay to heart. Just as fast as you will prove before your God that you are worthy to receive the mysteries, if you please to call them so, of the kingdom of heaven—that you are full of confidence in God—that you will never betray a thing that God tells you—that you will never reveal to your neighbour that which ought not to be revealed, as quick as you prepare to be entrusted with the things of

God, there is an eternity of them to bestow upon you. Instead of pleading with the Lord to bestow more upon you, plead with yourselves to have confidence in yourselves, to have integrity in yourselves, and know when to speak and what to speak, what to reveal, and how to carry yourselves and walk before the Lord. And just as fast as you prove to Him that you will preserve everything secret that ought to be—that you will deal out to your neighbours all which you ought, and no more, and learn how to dispense your knowledge to your families, friends, neighbours, and brethren, the Lord will bestow upon you, and give to you."[14]

Stand as Witnesses of God

Although it may not be wise to reveal what we learn from personal revelation, the fact that we receive revelation from God ought to humble us and motivate us to stand as witnesses of his blessings: "And it shall come to pass, that if you shall ask the Father in my name, in faith believing, you shall receive the Holy Ghost, which giveth utterance, that you may stand as a witness of the things of which you shall both hear and see" (D&C 14:8). When God shares a witness with us, he expects us to stand as witnesses for him "at all times and in all things, and in all places that [we] may be in" (Mosiah 18:9). We are expected to live to the best of our ability what we know to be true. "Therefore let your light so shine before this people, that they may see your good works and glorify your Father who is in heaven" (3 Nephi 12:16).

Line upon Line

The Prophet Joseph learned that the Lord will not give us everything all at once. He gives "the faithful line upon line, precept upon precept; and I will try you and prove you herewith" (D&C 98:12). The Lord has said he will hold some things in reserve until his second coming: "Yea, verily I say unto you, in that day when the Lord shall come, he shall reveal all things—things which have passed, and hidden things which no man knew, things of the earth, by which it was made, and the purpose and the end thereof—Things most precious, things that are above, and things that are beneath, things that are in the earth, and upon the earth, and in heaven" (D&C 101:32–34). One day, he has promised, he will reveal all things to us by the power of the Holy Ghost (D&C 121:26–30). "For behold, thus saith the Lord God: I will give unto the children of men line upon line, precept upon precept, here a little and there a little; and blessed are those who hearken unto my precepts, and lend an ear unto my counsel, for they shall learn wisdom" (2 Nephi 28:30).

There were times when the Prophet Joseph wished he could tell the Saints more of the great things of God, but their hearts were not prepared to receive them. Once in conversation with the Brethren, Joseph smote himself upon the chest and said, "I would to God that I could unbosom my feelings in the house of my friends."[15] His whole desire was to share what he had been privileged to see: "It is my meditation all the day, and more than my meat and drink, to know how I shall make the Saints of God to comprehend the visions that roll like an overflowing surge before my mind."[16] But he knew that care must be exercised. The Lord reveals to each nation and age what he knows they need: "For behold, the Lord doth grant unto all nations, of their own nation and tongue, to teach his word, yea, in wisdom, all that he seeth fit that they should have; therefore we see that the Lord doth counsel in wisdom, according to that which is just and true" (Alma 29:8).

The Prophet Joseph Smith gave us an abundance of instruction regarding the principles of personal revelation. We owe him an immense debt of gratitude. We are forever grateful to the Lord for this knowledge and for the spiritual safeguards against deception, which he also revealed to the Prophet Joseph Smith.

Notes

1. Smith, *Teachings*, 274.
2. Smith, *Teachings*, 61.

3. Smith, *Teachings*, 21.
4. Smith, *Teachings*, 215.
5. Packer, *Ensign*, November 1989, 15.
6. Oaks, "Revelation," 25.
7. Smith, *History of the Church*, 5:136.
8. Kimball, *Teachings of Spencer W. Kimball*, 402.
9. Nelson, *Young Woman's Journal*, 17 (1906): 543.
10. Hinckley, Conference Report, October 1967, 89.
11. Smith, *Teachings*, 195.
12. Smith, *History of the Church*, 6:244.
13. Packer, "Candle of the Lord," 53.
14. Young, *Journal of Discourses*, 4:371–72.
15. Woodruff, *Journal of Discourses*, 21:317.
16. Smith, *Teachings*, 296.

CHAPTER 11

Spiritual Safeguards

Like the iron rod along the path leading to eternal life, the Lord has placed some spiritual guardrails around the principle of revelation. They keep us from wandering into forbidden paths, keep us from falling into sin, and keep us on the strait and narrow path leading to greater light (1 Nephi 8:19–20). The following principles come from Joseph Smith's teachings and from the scriptures revealed to him. All of them are fundamental to spiritual safety. They can help us be more aware of the boundaries and spiritual safeguards the Lord has placed around personal revelation. Only those who are not deceived will abide the day and be prepared for the coming of the Lord (D&C 45:57).

Steadying the Ark

No bishop or any other ward or stake officer has the right to set aside part of the official program of the Church or bring in something else as a substitute. When Bishop Edward Partridge was called to preside over the Saints in Missouri, he altered the Lord's revealed order of inheritances in Zion. In response, the Lord sent a revelation to Bishop Partridge through the Prophet Joseph Smith: "I, the Lord God, will send one mighty and strong, holding the scepter of power in his hand, clothed with light for a covering, whose mouth shall utter words, eternal words; while his bowels shall be a fountain of truth, to set in order the house of God, and to arrange by lot the inheritances of the saints whose names are found, and the names of their fathers, and of their children, enrolled in the book of the law of God; while that man, who was called of God and appointed, that putteth forth his hand to steady the ark of God, shall fall by the shaft of death, like as a tree that is smitten by the vivid shaft of lightning" (D&C 85:7–8). Bishop Partridge repented and was not replaced. But since that time, self-vaunting individuals have used this revelation to claim that the Church today has gone astray and needs "one mighty and strong" to set it in order.

To "steady the ark" is to reach out, to exceed one's authority or responsibility in the Church to correct what one mistakenly thinks needs to be fixed. This phrase comes from the Old Testament account of the children of Israel returning the ark of the covenant to Jerusalem. The Lord had commanded that no one was to touch the ark, but the ox-cart was jostled, and "Uzzah put forth his hand to the ark of God, and took hold of it [to steady it]; for the oxen shook it" (2 Samuel 6:6). He was immediately smitten by the Lord and died. He had done precisely what he was not authorized to do.

Today the ark of the covenant, or the "ark of safety," is the restored gospel of Jesus Christ.[1] Christ stands at the head of the Church that bears his name (3 Nephi 27:8). If course corrections are needed, Elder Neal A. Maxwell observed, "this is something the Lord seems quite able to manage without requiring a host of helpers."[2]

If there are bumps in the road the Church has to pass over, it is not the members' place to attempt to steady the ark. God has called and empowered apostles and a prophet who have "power and authority over all the offices in the church in all ages of the world" (D&C 107:8). As Uzzah died physically, those who try to steady the ark today die spiritually. Elder Boyd K. Packer observed: "There are those within the Church who are disturbed when changes are made with which they disagree or when changes they propose are not made. They point to these as evidence that the leaders are not inspired. They write and speak to convince others that the doctrines and decisions of the Brethren are not given through inspiration. Two things characterize them: they are always irritated by the word *obedience*, and always they question revelation. It has always been so. Helaman described those who 'began to disbelieve in the spirit of prophecy and in the spirit of revelation; and the judgments of God did stare them in the face.' (Hel. 4:23.) 'They were left in their own strength' (v. 13), and 'the Spirit of the Lord did no more preserve them; yea, it had withdrawn from them' (v. 24)."[3]

President David O. McKay noted how quickly those who criticize the Church and its leaders lose the Spirit: "Their souls become embittered, their minds distorted, their judgment faulty, and their spirit depressed. Such is the pitiable condition of men who, neglecting their own responsibilities, spend their time in finding fault with others."[4]

President Harold B. Lee gave this wise counsel about avoiding deception: "The Lord has very plainly set forth a test by which anyone may challenge any and all who may come claiming, clandestinely, to have received some kind of priesthood authority. Now this is what the Lord said in the 42nd section of the Doctrine and Covenants, verse 11: 'Again, I say unto you, that it shall not be given to any one to go forth to preach my gospel, or to build up my church, except he be ordained by someone who has authority, and it is known to the church that he has authority and has been regularly ordained by the heads of the church.' Now, if one comes claiming that he has authority, ask him, 'Where do you get your authority? Have you been ordained by someone who has authority, who is known to the Church, that you have authority and have been regularly ordained by the heads of the Church?' If the answer is no, you may know that he is an imposter. This is the test that our people should always apply when some imposter comes trying to lead them astray."[5]

Revelation Leads to God

The purpose of revelation is to help us become like God. Revelation and the scriptures, the Prophet Joseph taught, "were given by direct inspiration for the good of man. We believe that God condescended to speak from the heavens and declare His will concerning the human family, to give them just and holy laws, to regulate their conduct, and guide them in a direct way, that in due time He might take them to Himself, and make them joint heirs with His Son."[6] If any revelation leads us away from the scriptures, from the prophets, or from the Church, we may know with surety it is not of God (Moroni 7:12–17; 1 John 4:1–3).

Angels and the Priesthood

Once priesthood keys and the Church have been established on the earth, not even angels from heaven will interfere with their functions. In Kirtland, Ohio, in Joseph Smith's day a man who wanted to be ordained a high priest was called on a mission and set apart as an elder. He had not been in the mission field very long before he began telling people he was a high priest. He was asked to produce a high priest's ordination certificate but could not do so. He claimed he was ordained to the office by an angel. When the news of his actions reached the Prophet Joseph, the man was immediately called home from his mission and questioned. Before long, the man confessed he had lied. "Brother Joseph observed to [the man] that he knew he had lied before he confessed it; that his declarations were not only false in themselves, but they involved a false principle. An angel, said Joseph, may administer the word of the Lord unto men, and bring intelligence to them from heaven upon various subjects; but no true angel from God will ever come to ordain any man, because they have once been sent to establish the priesthood by ordaining me thereunto; and the priesthood being once established on earth, with power to ordain others, no heavenly messenger will ever come to interfere with that power by ordaining any more. He referred to the angel that came to Cornelius and told Cornelius to send for Peter; but if there had been no Peter with keys and power to administer, the angel might have done it himself; but as there was, the angel would not interfere. Saul was directed to go to Ananias for instruction and to be administered to by him; but if there had been no Ananias with power and authority on the earth to administer in the name of Christ, the Lord might have done it himself. You may therefore know, from this time forward, that if any man comes to you professing to be ordained by an angel, he is either a liar or has been imposed upon in consequence of transgression by an angel of the devil, for this priesthood shall never be taken away from this church."[7]

Often those who leave the Church to begin their own organizations claim to have received their authority from a heavenly messenger. Those claims are simply not true. As Joseph Smith taught, no angel will ever interfere with the established order of the priesthood already on the earth.

Discerning False Spirits

The Prophet Joseph taught that only intelligence or revelation "which God alone could impart [is needed] to detect false spirits, and to prove what spirits were of God."[8] The things of God can only be known by the Spirit of God (1 Corinthians 2:11; Alma 5:46). "The Egyptians were not able to discover the difference between the miracles of Moses and those of the magicians until they came to be tested together; and if Moses had not appeared in their midst, they would unquestionably have thought that the miracles of the magicians were performed through the mighty power of God, for they were great miracles that were performed by them—a supernatural agency was developed, and great power manifested."[9] Who can detect Satan's influence, "or who can drag into daylight . . . false spirits that so frequently are made manifest among the Latter-day Saints? We answer that no man can do this without the Priesthood, and having a knowledge of the laws by which spirits are governed."[10]

Joseph Smith taught that "there always did, in every age, seem to be a lack of intelligence pertaining to this subject." Because men are ignorant of the nature and operations of the Spirit, they "imagine that when there is anything like power, revelation, or vision manifested, that it must be of God. . . . Nothing is a greater injury to the children of men than to be under the influence of a false spirit when they think they have the Spirit of God. . . . [And] unless some person or persons have a communication, or revelation from God, unfolding to them the operation of the spirit, they must eternally remain ignorant of these principles."[11]

Joseph testified that the apostles, who hold the keys of the priesthood (which includes the keys of the knowledge of God; see D&C 84:19) are therefore "enabled to unlock and unravel all things pertaining to the government of the Church, the welfare of society, the future destiny of men, and the agency, power and influence of spirits."[12] He said that "wicked spirits have their bounds, limits, and laws by which they are governed or controlled . . . and, it is very evident that they possess a power that none but those who have the Priesthood can control."[13] The authority of the priesthood, which modern apostles hold, is essential for spiritual progress and protection. Without it, we may be deceived by any display of supernatural power. Joseph declared: "No man nor sect of men without the regular constituted authorities, the Priesthood and discerning of spirits, can tell true from false spirits."[14]

Dignity and Decorum

Joseph Smith gave four grand keys by which the workings of the Spirit of God can be distinguished from the influence of Satan:

First, pure intelligence will be communicated by God's Spirit to further God's work. If "all the intelligence that can be obtained from [someone claiming to have the power of the Spirit] when they arise, is a shout of 'glory,' or 'hallelujah,' or some incoherent expression . . . surely, such a heterogeneous mass of confusion never can enter into the kingdom of heaven."[15]

Second, there is a dignity associated with the Spirit. There will never be anything "indecorous in the proceeding of the Lord's prophets in any age." "Strange fits, as in tremblings and faintings, which [make] them stretch out their legs and arms, as in a swoon; [remaining] awhile in trances, and coming out of them, . . . twitchings, tumblings" are not from God.[16] "God never had any prophets that acted in this way."[17]

Third, there is "nothing unnatural in the Spirit of God."

Extravagant revelations, speaking in a "muttering voice," or an unnatural voice, and their "bodies be[ing] distorted," are not of God,[18] Joseph taught. "Soon after the Gospel was established in Kirtland, and during the absence of the authorities of the Church, many false spirits were introduced, many strange visions were seen, and wild, enthusiastic notions were entertained; men ran out of doors under the influence of this spirit, and some of them got upon the stumps of trees and shouted, and all kinds of extravagances were entered into by them; one man pursued a ball that he said he saw flying in the air, until he came to a precipice, when he jumped into the top of a tree, which saved his life; and many ridiculous things were entered into, calculated to bring disgrace upon the Church of God, to cause the Spirit of God to be withdrawn, and to uproot and destroy those glorious principles which had been developed for the salvation of the human family. But when the authorities returned, the spirit was made manifest, those members that were exercised with it were tried for their fellowship, and those that would not repent and forsake it were cut off."[19]

Bishop Newel K. Whitney had difficulty controlling the people who were giving themselves up to these rather bizarre outbursts. One young woman who was eyewitness to the events said, "When the Prophet returned and learned the condition, he called a meeting in a little school house on Isaac Morley's farm. Joseph arose and said in a powerful voice, 'Let the spirits be made manifest.' Immediately, some began to sing, some to shout, some to cry, etc. When Joseph rebuked them, all became quiet except two, whom he rebuked separately."[20] Another young woman, Mary Elizabeth Rollins Lightner said of the events in Kirtland, "The Prophet Joseph Smith arrived in Kirtland, and moved into a part of Newel K. Whitney's house. . . . He came in time to rebuke the evil spirits, and set the Church in order. We all felt that he was a man of God, for he spoke with power, and as one having authority in very deed."[21]

Fourth, "there have also been ministering angels in the Church which were of Satan appearing as an angel of light."[22] Devils are quite willing to teach a few truths in order to promote falsehoods. But no angel from God, Joseph said, will ever contradict a former revelation.[23]

Little wonder the Lord has referred to Satan as the "father of all lies" (2 Nephi 2:18). He constantly contradicts former revelations from God.

Being Choosy about What God Reveals

Revelations from God are not served cafeteria style. We don't pick and choose which ones we like and which ones we don't. The Prophet Joseph said, "I believe all that God ever revealed, and I never heard of a man being damned for believing too much; but they are damned for unbelief."[24] "We believe," Joseph wrote, "all that God has revealed, all that He does now reveal, and we believe that He will yet reveal many great and important things pertaining to the Kingdom of God" (Article of Faith 9).

Following the Brethren

Those who try to run faster than they are sent will lose the Spirit. Personal revelations do not carry with them any implied authority. The Nephites, for example, tried to live a law without being authorized by the Lord or his prophets. They were severely rebuked and called to repentance (Jacob 2:23–26). As Joseph Smith explained, "Everything that God gives us is lawful and right; and it is proper that we should enjoy His gifts and blessings whenever and wherever He is disposed to bestow; but if we should seize upon those same blessings and enjoyments without law, without revelation, without commandment, those blessings and enjoyments would prove cursings and vexations in the end, and we should have to lie down in sorrow and wailings of everlasting regret. But in obedience there is joy and peace unspotted, unalloyed. . . . [God] says: 'Ask and ye shall receive, seek and ye shall find;' but, if you will take that which is not your own, or which I have not given you, you shall be rewarded according to your deeds."[25]

Those who try to run ahead of Church leaders will find that their efforts lead only to embarrassment and spiritual impoverishment.

Contention Hinders Revelation

We simply cannot hate our brother (or ward member) and love God at the same time (1 John 2:11; 4:20). "For verily, verily I say unto you, he that hath the spirit of contention is not of me, but is of the devil, who is the father of contention, and he stirreth up the hearts of men to contend with anger, one with another" (3 Nephi 11:29). "Therefore, if ye shall come unto me, or shall desire to come unto me, and rememberest that thy brother hath aught against thee—Go thy way unto thy brother, and first be reconciled to thy brother, and then come unto me with full purpose of heart, and I will receive you" (3 Nephi 12:23–24).

Sensationalism and Emotionalism

A most important revelation Joseph Smith received for the Church at Kirtland contained this declaration: "And the Spirit shall be given unto you by the prayer of faith; and if ye receive not the Spirit ye shall not teach" (D&C 42:14). When the Spirit is not present, not only should we not teach but we cannot teach. Spiritual learning does not occur without the Spirit. Joseph Smith said, "All are to preach the Gospel, by the power and influence of the Holy Ghost; and no man can preach the Gospel without the Holy Ghost."[26]

In the days of Joseph Smith, one brother preached and commanded others with "an authoritative voice and gesticulation, which [were] not according to the meekness of the spirit of Jesus. . . . Pride had engendered in [his] heart a desire to excel, and the spirit of meekness was withdrawn." This was a good man who got carried away with emotion when he taught. In a discussion about this man's loud and dramatic delivery, "President Oliver Cowdery arose, and . . . showed that a man might be highly excited and yet neither have the Spirit of God nor the spirit of Satan; but it came by his own spirit and judgment; therefore some things may be of God, others of men, and others from the adversary." Oliver pointed out that the man in question was not an evil man and that he had some of the Spirit in his sermon but that in "his own spirit of justification and pride" he had lost the Spirit of the Lord.

The Prophet Joseph confirmed that this man had erred in judgment and in spirit and was "not . . . sufficiently humble to deliver just the message that was required, and so he stumbled and could not get the Spirit, and the brethren were not edified, and he did not do the thing that God required." He continued, saying that the man had "erred in choosing words to communicate his thoughts . . . and that in all this, [he had] not designed to do wickedly, but he erred in judgment." Fortunately, the man acknowledged his mistakes and promised to comply with the counsel he was given to preach humbly, by the Spirit.[27]

Joseph had earlier counseled the elders who were to serve missions not to use a "hellfire and damnation" approach in preaching the gospel: "Brethren, as stars of the ensign which is now set up for the benefit of all nations, you are to enlighten the world, you are to prepare the way for the people to come up to Zion; you are to instruct men how to receive the fulness of the Gospel, and the everlasting covenants, even them that were from the beginning; you are to carry the ark of safety before the wondering multitudes, without fear, entreating and beseeching all men to be saved; you are to set an example of meekness and humility before Saints and sinners, as did the Savior; and when reviled you are not to revile again; you are to reason with men, as in days of old, to bear patiently and answer as the spirit of truth shall direct, allowing all credit for every item of good. You are to walk in the valley of humility, and pray for the salvation of all; yes, you are to pray for your enemies; and warn in compassion without threatening the wicked with judgments which are to be poured out upon the world hereafter. You have no right to take the judgments, which fell upon the ungodly before the flood, and pour them upon the head of this generation; you have no authority to use the judgments which God sent upon Pharaoh in Egypt, to terrify the inhabitants of America, neither have you any direction by commandment, to collect the calamities of six thousand years and paint them upon the curtain of these last days to scare mankind to repentance; no, you are to preach the Gospel, which is the power of God unto salvation, even glad tidings of great joy unto all people."[28]

Fanaticism and sensationalism in teaching the gospel are to be avoided. Said the Prophet Joseph: "A man came to me in Kirtland, and told me he had seen an angel, and described his dress. I told him he had seen no angel, and that there was no such dress in heaven. He grew mad, and went into the street and commanded fire to come down out of heaven to consume me. I laughed at him, and said, You are one of Baal's prophets; your God does not hear you; jump up and cut yourself; and he commanded fire from heaven to consume my house."[29]

When a person speaks or teaches by the power of the Spirit, he or she invites the Holy Ghost so that personal messages from God may be given to those being taught. Sensational storytelling or emotional appeals can never replace the power of the Spirit. Elder Loren C. Dunn has instructed that to "teach by the Spirit is not just a matter of telling inspirational stories or relaying experiences that appeal to the emotions. It is much more than this. In fact, some might confuse an emotional appeal with the gentle working of the Holy Spirit, but they are not necessarily the same. The quiet, peaceful confirmation that comes into one's heart as he is being taught by a faithful teacher may not be emotional at all in terms of what the world might call an emotional experience. But it will edify or spiritually uplift the teacher and the student. Both will rejoice as they learn and relearn spiritual truths. 'Behold, I will tell you in your mind and in your heart,' and 'you shall feel that it is right.'"[30]

Elder Howard W. Hunter said: "Let me offer a word of caution on this subject. I think if we are not careful . . . we may begin to try to counterfeit the true influence of the Spirit of the Lord by unworthy and manipulative means. I get concerned when it appears that strong emotion or free-flowing tears are equated with the presence of the Spirit. Certainly the Spirit of the Lord can bring strong emotional feelings, including tears, but that outward manifestation ought not to be confused with the presence of the Spirit itself. . . . Sometimes [manifestations of the Spirit] are accompanied by total silence. Other times they are accompanied by joy. Always they are accompanied by a great manifestation of the truth, of revelation to the heart."[31]

Unsubstantiated rumors and loose writings that are intended to sensationalize the gospel are also not conducive to the Spirit. President Harold B. Lee commented more than once in general conference on such pseudospirituality: "It never ceases to amaze me how gullible some of our Church members are in broadcasting sensational stories, or dreams, or visions, or purported patriarchal blessings, or quotations, or supposedly from some person's private diary. . . .

"And yet the amazing thing is that we find that these spurious writings and some of these purported revelations, which we found upon investigation are absolutely false, are finding their way into our Relief Society meetings, into priesthood quorums, firesides, institutes, and seminaries."[32]

President Lee also declared: "As I say, it never ceases to amaze me how gullible some of our Church members are at broadcasting these sensational stories, or dreams, or visions, some alleged to have been given to Church leaders, past or present, supposedly from some person's private diary, without first verifying the report with proper Church authorities.

"If our people want to be safely guided during these troublous times of deceit and false rumors, they must follow their leaders and seek for the guidance of the Spirit of the Lord in order to avoid falling prey to clever manipulators who, with cunning sophistry, seek to draw attention and gain a following to serve their own notions and sometimes sinister motives."[33]

Seeking for a Sign

The Lord explained to the Prophet Joseph Smith that those who seek for signs may receive them, but signs will not bring about salvation. There have always been sign-seekers in the Church, even from the beginning. Faith does not come from signs, but signs confirm the faith of righteous people. Even when faith is evidenced, signs come only by the will of God, not as man desires (D&C 63:7–10). Some who lack faith may see signs but only "in wrath unto their condemnation" (D&C 63:11). "Wherefore, I, the Lord, am not pleased with those among you who have sought after signs and wonders" (D&C 63:12).

During his earthly ministry the Savior said, "A wicked and adulterous generation seeketh after a sign" (Matthew 16:4). The Prophet shared an experience that illustrates the Savior's teaching: "When I was preaching in Philadelphia, a Quaker called out for a sign. I told him to be still. After the sermon, he again asked for a sign. I told the congregation the man was an adulterer; that a wicked and adulterous generation seeketh after a sign; and that the Lord had said to me in a revelation, that any man who wanted a sign was an adulterous person. 'It is true,' cried one, 'for I caught him in the very act,' which the man afterwards confessed when he was baptized."[34]

The Prophet Joseph taught, "I will give you one of the Keys of the mysteries of the Kingdom. It is an eternal principle, that has existed with God from all eternity: That man who rises up to condemn others, finding fault with the Church, saying that they are out of the way, while he himself is righteous, then know assuredly, that that man is in the high road to apostasy; and if he does not repent, will apostasize, as God lives. The principle is as correct as the one that Jesus put forth in saying that he who seeketh a sign is an adulterous person; and that principle is eternal, undeviating, and firm as the pillars of heaven; for whenever you see a man seeking after a sign, you may set it down that he is an adulterous man."[35]

President John Taylor once said, "[I am reminded] of a remark made once in Far West by a man; says he, 'I know Joseph Smith is a false Prophet, and that the Book of Mormon and Covenants are false.' How do you know it. 'Why, says he, if a man commit adultery, he shall apostatize; and I have done it, and have not apostatized.' That is a good sample of the intelligence that is manifested by many. Do people think they can commit acts of iniquity, transgress the laws of God, and break their covenants, after being admitted to great privileges in the kingdom of God, and retain His Spirit, and a knowledge of His purposes?"[36]

False Traditions

In the Book of Mormon and in the Doctrine and Covenants, the Prophet Joseph was told that false traditions can impair our ability to receive revelation (Mosiah 1:5; Alma 9:16–17; Helaman 15:7–8; D&C 93:36–40). He said, "There are those who profess to be Saints who are too apt to murmur, and find fault, when any advice is given, which comes in opposition to their feelings, even when they, themselves, ask for counsel; much more so when counsel is given unasked for, which does not agree with their notion of things; but brethren, we hope for better things from the most of you; we trust that you desire counsel, from time to time, and that you will cheerfully conform to it, whenever you receive it from a proper source."[37]

Tradition often keeps people from investigating the restored gospel: "It is very difficult for us to communicate to the churches all that God has revealed to us, in consequence of tradition; for we are differently situated from any other people that ever existed upon this earth."[38] That is precisely the reason other Christian churches believe that Latter-day Saints are not Christian—because we do not trace our doctrines and beliefs to the traditions and creeds formulated hundreds of years after Christ's death.

False traditions can cause individual hearts to be closed to new truths. Elder George A. Smith, an apostle, recalled an incident when a "very zealous" member tried to have Joseph Smith tried in a bishop's council. The charge was that Joseph had not prohibited the aged sisters from wearing caps, nor the men from wearing little cushions on their coat sleeves (being fashionable at the time to do so). Elder George A. Smith said, "That man was possessed of such wisdom as man could reasonably manifest, yet he was so perfectly full of folly and of his own traditions and notions he had fancied over in his own head, that seemingly it was impossible for him to understand anything better; he was blinded, and lifted his hand against the Prophet of God.'" Soon thereafter the man lost his standing in the Church.

The Prophet Joseph once lamented: "I have tried for a number of years to get the minds of the Saints prepared to receive the things of God; but we frequently see some of them, after suffering all they have for the work of God, will fly to pieces like glass as soon as anything comes that is contrary to their traditions: they cannot stand the fire at all. How many will be able to abide a celestial law, and go through and receive their exaltation, I am unable to say, as many are called, but few are chosen."[39]

On another occasion the Prophet said: "All are bound by the principles of virtue and happiness, but one great privilege of the Priesthood is to obtain revelations of the mind and will of God. . . . If the Church knew all the commandments, one half they would condemn through prejudice and ignorance."[40] Phrases like "That's not how we've done it before," or "That's not how we did it when _____ was the president" can prevent us from receiving modern revelation. "As we lay off our false traditions and foolish notions," Brigham Young taught, "we receive more and more light, and thus we grow in grace."[41]

Wilford Woodruff recorded his views about what happened to those who refused to let go of false traditions: "I have seen men in the days of Joseph bring up principles, and read, and teach, and advocate theories, when the Prophet would say, 'It is not right to do so: they are not true.' Those men would still argue, maintain their position, and they would write in defence of their theories when the Prophet condemned them, and they would say, 'We have no faith in your theory, nor in the system you present.' The very moment a man does that, he crosses the path of the servant of God who is set to lead the way to life and salvation. This is one thing that the Elders should carefully avoid. The fact is, there are a great many things taught in the building up of this kingdom which seem strange to us, being contrary to our traditions, and are calculated to try men. Brother Joseph used a great many methods of testing the integrity of men; and he taught a great many things which, in consequence of tradition, required prayer, faith, and a testimony from the Lord, before they could be believed by many of the Saints. His mind was opened by the visions of the Almighty, and the Lord taught him many things by vision and revelation that were never taught publicly in his days; for the people could not bear the flood of intelligence which God poured into his mind."[42]

Notes

1. Smith, *History of the Church*, 1:280.
2. Maxwell, *Ensign*, May 1982, 39.
3. Packer, *Ensign*, November 1989, 15.
4. McKay, Conference Report, April 1936, 60.
5. Lee, "Admonitions for the Priesthood of God," 106.
6. Smith, *Teachings*, 53–54.
7. *Millennial Star*, 20 November 1846, 139.
8. Smith, *Teachings*, 202.
9. Smith, *Teachings*, 202.
10. Smith, *Teachings*, 204–5.
11. Smith, *Teachings*, 203, 205.
12. Smith, *Teachings*, 206.
13. Smith, *Teachings*, 208.
14. Smith, *Teachings*, 213.
15. Smith, *Teachings*, 204.
16. Smith, *Teachings*, 209.
17. Smith, *Teachings*, 209.
18. Smith, *Teachings*, 214.
19. Smith, *Teachings*, 213–14.
20. Lucy Morley Allen, *Young Woman's Journal* 17 (December 1906): 537–38, as cited in Andrus and Andrus, *They Knew the Prophet*, 31–32.
21. Lightner, "Mary Elizabeth Rollins Lightner," *Utah Genealogical and Historical Magazine*, 17 (July 1926): 194–95.
22. Smith, *Teachings*, 214.
23. Smith, *Teachings*, 214–15.
24. Smith, *History of the Church*, 6:477.
25. Smith, *History of the Church*, 5:135–36.
26. Smith, *Teachings*, 112.
27. Smith, *History of the Church*, 2:278–80.
28. Smith, *History of the Church*, 1:280.
29. Smith, *History of the Church*, 5:267–68.
30. Dunn, "Teaching by the Power of the Spirit," 11.
31. Hunter, "Eternal Investments," 3.
32. Lee, Conference Report, April 1970, 55–56.

33. Lee, "Admonitions for the Priesthood of God," 105–6.
34. Smith, *Teachings*, 278.
35. Taylor, *Journal of Discourses*, 1:372.
36. Smith, *Teachings*, 156–57.
37. Smith, *History of the Church*, 4:45.
38. Smith, *Teachings*, 70.
39. Smith, *Teachings*, 331.
40. Smith, *Teachings*, 111.
41. Young, *Journal of Discourses*, 2:315–316.
42. Woodruff, *Journal of Discourses*, 5:84–85.

CHAPTER 12

Gratitude for the Prophet Joseph Smith

Joseph Smith was constantly persecuted from the moment he announced he had seen God the Father and his Son, Jesus Christ, until his death twenty-four years later. "Why was he hunted from neighborhood to neighborhood, from city to city, from state to state, and at last suffered death?" President Brigham Young explained: "Because he received revelations from the Father, from the Son, and was ministered to by holy angels, and published to the world the direct will of the Lord concerning his children on the earth. Again, why was he persecuted? Because he revealed to all mankind a religion so plain and so easily understood, consistent with the Bible, and so true."[1]

Many in his day were quick to seize on any minor imperfection of Joseph Smith's character. But from the temple in Nauvoo, one month before his martyrdom, Joseph testified: "When did I ever teach anything wrong from this stand? When was I ever confounded? . . . I never told you I was perfect—but there is no error in the revelations which I have taught."[2]

The world owes Joseph Smith a debt of gratitude for the truths and ordinances he restored. Every person on earth is indebted to him, yet the Lord warned him that many would despise him: "The ends of the earth shall inquire after thy name, and fools shall have thee in derision, and hell shall rage against thee; while the pure in heart, and the wise, and the noble, and the virtuous, shall seek counsel, and authority, and blessings constantly from under thy hand. And thy people shall never be turned against thee by the testimony of traitors" (D&C 122:1–3).

An experience the Prophet Joseph had near Washington D.C. illustrates the debt owed to him and how the world generally responds to him. Shortly after the Saints settled in Commerce, Illinois (which Joseph Smith later named *Nauvoo*, "the city beautiful"), a committee was organized to present petitions detailing the Saints' sufferings and losses during the Missouri persecutions. At the October 1839 general conference, Judge Elias Higbee was assigned to accompany Joseph Smith and his counselor in the First Presidency, Sidney Rigdon, to Washington, D.C. At Springfield, Illinois, the Prophet preached several times, and eager listeners joined the Church as a result of the spiritual experiences attending the Prophet's preaching.

The committee continued their journey to Washington by way of Columbus, Ohio, where Sidney Rigdon, too ill to travel any further, was left under the care of a doctor. The others continued to Washington by stagecoach. The Prophet Joseph described what happened: "While on the mountains some distance from Washington, our coachman stepped into a public house to take his grog, when the horses took fright and ran down the hill at full speed. I persuaded my fellow travelers to be quiet and retain their seats, but had to hold one woman to prevent her throwing her infant out of the coach. The passengers were exceedingly agitated, but I used every persuasion to calm their feelings; and opening the door, I secured my hold on the side of the coach the best way I could, and succeeded in placing myself in the coachman's seat, and reining up the horses, after they had run some two or three miles, and neither coach, horses, or passengers received any injury. My course was spoken of in the highest terms of commendation, as being one of the most daring and heroic deeds, and no language could express the gratitude of the passengers, when they found themselves safe, and the horses quiet. There were some members of Congress with us, who proposed naming the incident to that body, believing they would reward such conduct by some public act; but on inquiring my name, to mention as the author of their safety, and finding it to be Joseph Smith the 'Mormon Prophet,' as they called me, I heard no more of their praise, gratitude, or reward."[3]

In a way, the Prophet Joseph Smith has done a similar thing for all of us—he has helped to save us. Without the revelations he received as the first prophet of the Restoration, mankind would still be lost in apostasy. No wonder John Taylor, at the time of Joseph's martyrdom, exclaimed: "Joseph Smith, the Prophet and Seer of the Lord, has done more, save Jesus only, for the salvation of men in this world, than any other man that ever lived in it. . . . [He] has sent the fulness of the everlasting gospel . . . to the four quarters of the earth; has brought forth the revelations and commandments . . . and many other wise documents and instructions for the benefit of the children of men; . . . and like most of the Lord's anointed in ancient time, has sealed his mission and his works with his own blood" (D&C 135:3).

Because of Joseph Smith's spirituality and faith, we enjoy the wonderful blessings of the Restoration. Because of the generous revelations from God through him, we have been blessed to know God, to know his Son, Jesus Christ, and to know how, through the Holy Ghost, to receive the individual revelation necessary to work our way through mortality and receive exaltation and eternal life.

On April 7, 1844, just two months before his martyrdom, the Prophet Joseph said: "If I had not experienced what I have, I could not have believed it myself. . . . I cannot lie down until all my work is finished. . . . When I am called by the trump of the archangel and weighed in the balance, you will all know me then. I add no more. God bless you all. Amen."[4]

President Brigham Young testified of the importance of Joseph's life and mission to every one of us: "Joseph Smith holds the keys of this last dispensation, and is now engaged behind the vail in the great work of the last days. . . . No man or woman in this dispensation will ever enter into the celestial kingdom of God without the consent of Joseph Smith. From the day that the Priesthood was taken from the earth to the winding-up scene of all things, every man and woman must have the certificate of Joseph Smith, junior, as a passport to their entrance into the mansion where God and Christ are—I with you and you with me. I cannot go there without his consent."[5]

Said President George Q. Cannon: "He [Joseph Smith] stands at the head. He is a unique character, differing from every other man in this respect, and excelling every other man. . . . He was faithful, and died faithful. He stands therefore at the head of this dispensation, and will throughout all eternity. . . . If we get our salvation we shall have to pass by him; if we enter into our glory it will be through the authority that he has received. We cannot get around him."[6]

President Gordon B. Hinckley added this testimony: "We do not worship the prophet, we worship God, our Eternal Father, and the risen Lord Jesus Christ. But we acknowledge him, . . . we reverence him as an instrument in the hands of the Almighty in restoring to the earth the ancient truths of the divine gospel, together with the priesthood through which the authority of God is exercised in the affairs of his church and for the blessing of his people."[7]

Choice Seer of the Lord

While most religionists were confused about revelation, or denying it, Joseph Smith was receiving it. While others were saying the canon of scripture was closed, Joseph Smith was receiving new scripture. While many Christian scholars have claimed that the book of Revelation is so full of symbolism as to be of little practical value, Joseph Smith declared, "The Book of Revelation is one of the plainest books God ever caused to be written."[8]

The things of the Spirit were easier for him to comprehend because these things were revealed to him. As early as March 1829 the Lord declared to the Prophet Joseph Smith: "This generation shall have my word through you" (D&C 5:10). At the time, Joseph Smith was twenty-three years of age. He would live only fifteen more years. But in those fifteen compressed years, Joseph Smith became the instrument through whom the Lord ushered in the final dispensation of the fulness of times, the dispensation in which all things "from the days of Adam even to the present time. . . . shall be revealed" (D&C 128:18, 20–21).

Note that the Lord said the Restoration would come *through*, not *from* or *by*, the Prophet Joseph (D&C 5:10). The Restoration is so grand in vision, so all-encompassing in thought and doctrine, so far beyond mortal power and authority, that it could not possibly have come *from* the Prophet Joseph Smith or *from* any other mortal. For more than seventeen hundred years, no person, no committee, no council, and no creed had been able to bring back the original Church with all its doctrines, priesthoods, and principles. Many individuals had recognized that doctrines and teachings were missing, but no individual nor any group of individuals was able to recover what was lost. The work of the Restoration was simply beyond human ability.

Even if Joseph Smith had been the most gifted linguist, the most learned biblical scholar, the most studied anthropologist, the most spiritual intellect on the face of the earth (which he did become as a result of being heaven-taught and angel-tutored), he still would not have been able to restore, on his own, the priesthood keys and authority that had been taken from the earth with the death of the early apostles. Priesthood authority can only be given by the laying on of hands by someone holding the proper authority. That is why Daniel, Peter, John the Beloved, and other prophets foretold the need for a latter-day restoration from heaven (D&C 65:2, 6; Daniel 2; Acts 3:19–21; Revelation 14:6–7).

Obtaining the Assurance of Salvation

The Prophet Joseph shared the gospel with his extended family as the work of the Restoration began to unfold. He wrote a letter from Kirtland, Ohio, to his uncle Silas, in which he bore witness of the revelations that God had previously given and of the modern revelation God was now sending. His clear and thoughtful testimony was that God loves his children and will send revelation to guide us all:

"If the saints, in the days of the apostles, were privileged to take the [earlier] saints for example, and lay hold of the same promises, and attain to the same exalted privileges of knowing that their names were written in the Lamb's Book of Life, and that they were sealed there as a perpetual memorial before the face of the Most High, *will not the same faithfulness, the same purity of heart, and the faith, bring the same assurance of eternal life, and that in the same manner to the children of men now, in this age of the world?* I have no doubt, but that the holy prophets, and apostles, and saints in ancient days were saved in the kingdom of God; neither do I doubt but that they held converse and communion with him while they were in the flesh, as Paul said to his Corinthian brethren, that the Lord Jesus showed himself to above five hundred saints at one time after his resurrection. Job said that he knew that his Redeemer lived, and that he should see him in the flesh in the latter days. I may believe that Enoch walked with God, and by faith was translated. I may believe that Noah was a perfect man in his generation, and also walked with God. I may believe that Abraham communed with God, and conversed with angels. I may believe that Isaac obtained a renewal of the covenant made to Abraham by the direct voice of the Lord. I may believe that Jacob conversed with holy angels, and heard the word of his Maker, that he wrestled with the angel until he prevailed, and obtained a blessing. I may believe that Elijah was taken to heaven in a chariot of fire with fiery horses. I may believe that the saints saw the Lord, and conversed with him face to face after his resurrection. I may believe that the Hebrew church came to Mount Zion, and unto the city of the living God, the heavenly Jerusalem, and to an innumerable company of angels. I may believe that they looked into eternity, and saw the Judge of all, and Jesus the Mediator of the New Covenant. But will all this purchase an assurance for me, and waft me to the regions of eternal day, with my garments spotless, pure and white? Or, must I not rather obtain for myself, by my own faith and diligence in keeping the commandments of the Lord, an assurance of salvation for myself? And *have I not an equal privilege with the ancient saints? And will not the Lord hear my prayers, and listen to my cries as soon as he ever did theirs, if I come to him in the manner they did?* Or, is he a respecter of persons?"[9]

The light within our souls is the light God has given to his children in all ages of time. When followed, it leads to blessings, covenants, and assurances that eternal life is within reach. Personal revelation is available to us all regardless of the place, race, or time in which we are born. The Savior invites us to come unto him, through his light and through the gifts and blessing of the Holy Ghost: "Learn of me . . . and ye shall find rest unto your souls" (Matthew 11:29); "I am come a light into the world, that whosoever believeth on me should not abide in darkness" (3 Nephi 15:9); "I am the light and the life of the world" (3 Nephi 9:18); "behold, I am the law, and the light. Look unto me, and endure to the end, and ye shall live" (3 Nephi 15:9); "behold I am the light; I have set an example for you" (3 Nephi 18:16); "therefore, hold up your light that it may shine unto the world. Behold I am the light which ye shall hold up—that which ye have seen me do" (3 Nephi 18:24).

"Praise to the Man"

Brigham Young said, "I feel like shouting hallelujah, all the time, when I think that I ever knew Joseph Smith, the Prophet whom the Lord raised up and ordained and to whom He gave keys and power to build up the kingdom of God on earth and sustain it. These keys are committed to this people and we have power to continue the work that Joseph commenced, until everything is prepared for the coming of the Son of Man. This is the business of the Latter-day Saints, and it is all the business we have on hand."[10]

The Prophet Joseph Smith was great because he did the work of our Heavenly Father, who said, "For behold, this is my work and my glory—to bring to pass the immortality and eternal life of man" (Moses 1:39). Leo Tolstoy commented on the genius of the Restoration, saying that the principles restored by Joseph Smith "teach people not only of heaven and its attendant glories, but how to live so that the social and economical relations with each other are placed on a sound basis. If the people follow the teachings of this Church nothing can stop their progress. It will be limitless. . . . There have been great movements started in the past, but they've died or been modified along the way, before they reach maturity. If Mormonism is able to endure, unmodified until it reaches the third and fourth generation, it is destined to become the greatest power the world has ever known."[11] And so it is!

Joseph Smith made a contribution to mankind greater than that of any theologian, scholar, or politician. In 1968 an editor for the *Toronto Star* wrote: "No matter what anyone might think of him, Joseph Smith the Mormon prophet was one of the most dynamic and creative men of the nineteenth century. In fact, he's one of a half dozen of the greatest men of that era."[12]

He was also great in the eyes of God. In 1844, when Lucy Mack Smith first saw the martyred bodies of her sons Hyrum and Joseph, she cried out, "My God, my God, why hast thou forsaken this family?" A voice replied, "I have taken them to myself, that they might have rest." She recorded, "As I looked on their peaceful, smiling countenances, I seemed almost to hear them say, 'Mother, weep not for us; we have overcome the world by love. We have carried them the gospel, that their souls might be saved; they slew us for our testimony, and thus placed us beyond their power; their ascendancy is for a moment; ours is an eternal triumph.'"[13]

Thousands attended the funeral of Joseph and Hyrum in Nauvoo. Brother William W. Phelps paid a final tribute to the Prophet with a poem: "Praise to the man who communed with Jehovah. Jesus anointed that prophet and seer." We might add our own declaration of gratitude: Praise to Jehovah and praise to the Father for communing with such great men, including all the prophets of the Restoration.

Joseph finished his work of laying the foundation of the Restoration. He restored the revealed, Spirit-filled principles and ordinances of the gospel of Jesus Christ. His teachings and experiences show how we can come to know for ourselves that the doctrines he taught are true. By learning to nurture and follow the light within, we too can receive heaven-sent revelations and assurances: "Yea, and cry unto God for all thy support; yea, let all thy doings be unto the Lord, and whithersoever thou goest let it be in the Lord; yea, let all thy thoughts be directed unto the Lord; yea, let the affections of thy heart be placed upon the Lord forever. Counsel with the Lord in all thy doings, and he will direct thee for good; yea, when thou liest down at night lie down unto the Lord, that he may watch over you in your sleep; and when thou risest in the morning let thy heart be full of thanks unto God; and if ye do these things, ye shall be lifted up at the last day" (Alma 37:36–37).

Then we, with the Prophet Joseph Smith, will be able to say from our own experience and from personal revelation, "When the light rested upon me, I saw" (Joseph Smith–History 1:17).

Notes

1. Young, *Journal of Discourses*, 18:231.
2. Smith, *Teachings*, 368.
3. Smith, *History of the Church*, 4:23.
4. Smith, *Teachings*, 361.
5. Young, *Journal of Discourses*, 7:289.
6. Cannon, *Journal of Discourses*, 23:361.
7. Hinckley, *Ensign*, May 1977, 65.
8. Smith, *Teachings*, 290.
9. Smith, *History of Joseph Smith*, 235–37; emphasis added.
10. Young, *Journal of Discourses*, 3:51.
11. Tolstoy, as cited in Haight, *Ensign*, May 1980, 11.
12. As cited in *Church News*, 2 March 1968, 6.
13. Smith, *History of Joseph Smith*, 324, 325.

Sources

"Although Dead, Yet He Speaketh." *Millennial Star* (20 November 1846).

Andrus, Hyrum L., and Helen Mae Andrus, comps. *They Knew the Prophet.* Salt Lake City: Deseret Book, 1999.

Arrington, Leonard J. *Brigham Young: American Moses.* New York: Alfred A. Knopf, 1985.

Asay, Carlos E. *Ensign*, November 1978.

Ashton, Marvin J. *Ensign*, November 1987.

———. *Ensign*, November 1992.

Ballard, M. Russell. *Ensign*, May 1998.

Bateman, Merrill J. "Brigham Young University in the New Millennium." Address delivered at the BYU Annual University Conference, 24 August 1998.

Benson, Ezra Taft. Conference Report, April 1965.

———. Conference Report, April 1986.

———. Conference Report, October 1986.

———. *Ensign*, May 1986.

———. *The Teachings of Ezra Taft Benson.* Salt Lake City: Bookcraft, 1988.

———. "What I Hope You Will Teach Your Children about the Temple." *Ensign*, August 1985.

———. *A Witness and a Warning.* Salt Lake City: Deseret Book, 1988.

———. "Fourteen Fundamentals in Following the Prophet." *BYU Speeches of the Year, 1980.* Provo: Brigham Young University Press, 1981.

Berrett, LaMar C. "An Impressive Letter from the Pen of Joseph Smith." *BYU Studies* 11, no. 3 (Spring 1971).

Black, Susan Easton, John Telford, and Kim C. Averett. *Navuoo.* Salt Lake City: Deseret Book, 1997.

Cannon, Donald Q., Larry E. Dahl, and John W. Welch. "The Restoration of

Major Doctrines through Joseph Smith: The Godhead, Mankind, and the Creation." *Ensign*, January 1989.

———. "Discourse by President George Q. Cannon." *Millennial Star*, 23 April 1894.

———. *Gospel Truth*. Selected by Jerreld L. Newquist. Salt Lake City: Deseret Book, 1987.

Children's Songbook. Salt Lake City: The Church of Jesus Christ of Latter-day Saints, 1989.

Church History in the Fulness of Times. Prepared by the Church Educational System. Salt Lake City: The Church of Jesus Christ of Latter-day Saints, 1989.

Church News, 2 March 1968.

Clark, J. Reuben, Jr. Conference Report, October 1936.

Croft, David. "Spare Time's Rare to Apostle." *Church News*, 24 January 1976.

Dahl, Larry E., and Charles D. Tate Jr. *Lectures on Faith in Historical Perspective*. Provo, Utah: Brigham Young University, 1990.

Dahl, Larry E., and Donald Q. Cannon. *The Teachings of Joseph Smith*. Salt Lake City: Bookcraft, 1997.

The Doctrine and Covenants Student Manual. Prepared by the Church Educational System. Salt Lake City: The Church of Jesus Christ of Latter-day Saints, 1981.

Dunn, Loren C. "Unity in the Faith." *Speeches of the Year, 1980*. Provo, Utah: Brigham Young University Press, 1981.

———. "Teaching by the Power of the Spirit." *Ensign*, September 1984.

Ehat, Andrew F., and Lyndon W. Cook, comps. *The Words of Joseph Smith*. Provo, Utah: Brigham Young University, 1980.

Eyring, Henry B. Conference Report, April 1996.

———. Conference Report, October 1996.

Faust, James E. *Ensign*, November 1994.

———. *To Reach Even unto You*. Salt Lake City: Deseret Book, 1980.

Featherstone, Vaughn J. *Man of Holiness*. Salt Lake City: Deseret Book, 1998.

Groberg, John H. "What Is Your Mission?" *Speeches of the Year, 1979*. Provo, Utah: Brigham Young University Press, 1980.

The Guide to the Scriptures. Salt Lake City: The Church of Jesus Christ of Latter-day Saints, 1993.

Haight, David B. *Ensign*, May 1980.

———. *Ensign*, November 1990.

Hall, Randall. "The Preeminence of Teaching and the Role of Religious Education in CES." Address delivered at the Book of Mormon Symposium, Provo, Utah, 12 August 1997.

Hinckley, Gordon B. Conference Report, October 1967.

———. *Ensign*, May 1977.

Holland, Jeffrey R. *Christ and the New Covenant*. Salt Lake City: Deseret Book, 1997.

Hunter, Howard W. "Eternal Investments." Address to religious educators, Salt Lake City, Utah, 10 February 1989.

Hymns of The Church of Jesus Christ of Latter-day Saints. Salt Lake City: The Church of Jesus Christ of Latter-day Saints, 1985.

Jessee, Dean C., ed. *The Personal Writings of Joseph Smith*. Salt Lake City: Deseret Book, 1984.

———. "Priceless Words and Fallible Memories." *BYU Studies*, Spring 1991.

Journal of Discourses. 26 vols. London: Latter-day Saints' Book Depot, 1854–86.

Kimball, J. Golden. Conference Report, April 1906.

Kimball, Sarah M. "Story of the Relief Society," *Relief Society Magazine*, March 1919.

Kimball, Spencer W. Conference Report, April 1977.

———. *Ensign*, November 1979.

———. "The Things of Eternity—Stand We in Jeopardy?" *Ensign*, January 1977.

———. *Teachings of Spencer W. Kimball*. Edited by Edward L. Kimball. Salt Lake City: Bookcraft, 1982.

———. "What I Hope You Will Teach My Grandchildren and All Others of the Youth of Zion." Address to seminary and institute personnel, 11 July 1966.

Larsen, Dean L. "'Prepare Ye for That Which Is to Come.'" *Doctrine and Covenants Symposium*. Provo, Utah: Brigham Young University, 1989.

LDS Collector's Library '97. CD-ROM. Salt Lake City: Infobases, 1997.

Lee, Harold B. "Admonitions for the Priesthood of God." *Ensign*, January 1973.

———. "BYU Commencement Address." 28 June 1955.

———. Conference Report, October 1964.

———. Conference Report, April 1970.

———. Conference Report, April 1971.

———. *Decisions for Successful Living*. Salt Lake City: Deseret Book, 1973.
———. *Improvement Era*, June 1970.
———. *Stand Ye in Holy Places: Selected Sermons and Writings of President Harold B. Lee*. Salt Lake City: Deseret Book, 1974.
———. *The Teachings of Harold B. Lee*. Edited by Clyde J. Williams. Salt Lake City: Bookcraft, 1966.
Lightner, Mary. "Mary Elizabeth Rollins Lightner." *Utah Genealogical and Historical Magazine* 17 (July 1926): 193–205, 250.
Marsh, W. Jeffrey. *Unto Us a Child Is Born*. Salt Lake City: Bookcraft, 1994.
Maxwell, Neal A. *Ensign*, November 1982.
———. *Ensign*, May 1982.
———. *Ensign*, May 1995.
———. *Even As I Am*. Salt Lake City: Deseret Book, 1982.
———. *Ensign*, May 1994.
———. *Ensign*, May 1985.
———. "Teaching by the Spirit—'The Language of Inspiration.'" In *Old Testament Symposium* (CES). Salt Lake City: The Church of Jesus Christ of Latter-day Saints, 1991.
McConkie, Bruce R. *Ensign*, November 1976.
———. *Doctrinal New Testament Commentary*. 3 vols. Salt Lake City: Bookcraft, 1995–73.
———. *Ensign*, May 1974.
———. "Holy Writ: Published Anew." Address delivered at Regional Representatives Seminar, 2 April 1982.
———. *The Millennial Messiah*. Salt Lake City: Deseret Book, 1982.
———. *Mormon Doctrine*. 2d ed. Salt Lake City: Bookcraft, 1966.
———. *The Mortal Messiah*. Salt Lake City: Deseret Book, 1980.
———. *A New Witness for the Articles of Faith*. Salt Lake City: Deseret Book, 1985.
———. *The Promised Messiah*. Salt Lake City: Deseret Book, 1981.
———. "What Does It Mean to Be Born Again?" *New Era*, August 1971.
McConkie, Joseph Fielding. *Here We Stand*. Salt Lake City: Deseret Book, 1995.
McKay, David O. Conference Report, April 1936.
———. Conference Report, April 1946.
———. *Gospel Ideals*. Salt Lake City: Improvement Era, 1953.
———. *Man May Know for Himself*. Salt Lake City: Deseret Book, 1967.

———. *True to the Faith*. Compiled by Llewelyn R. McKay. Salt Lake City: Bookcraft, 1966.

———. *Millennial Star*, 20 November 1846, 139.

Nelson, William G. *Young Woman's Journal* 17 (1906).

Norton, Don. "I Have a Question." *Ensign*, August 1978.

Oaks, Dallin H. "Revelation." *Speeches of the Year*. Provo, Utah: Brigham Young University Publications, 1982.

———. "Spiritual Gifts." In *A Heritage of Faith: Talks Selected from the BYU Women's Conferences*. Salt Lake City: Deseret Book, 1988.

———. *Ensign*, November 1994.

Pace, Glenn L. *Ensign*, November 1992.

Packer, Boyd K. "The Candle of the Lord." *Ensign*, January 1983.

———. *Ensign*, May 2000.

———. *The Holy Temple*. Salt Lake City: Bookcraft, 1980.

———. *Ensign*, November 1994.

———. *Ensign*, November 1979.

———. *Ensign*, November 1989.

———. *That All May Be Edified*. Salt Lake City: Bookcraft, 1982.

Pratt, Orson. *Masterful Discourses and Writings of Orson Pratt*. Salt Lake City: Bookcraft, 1962.

———. *A Series of Pamphlets*. Liverpool: Franklin D. Richards, 1852.

Pratt, Parley P. *Autobiography of Parley P. Pratt*. Salt Lake City: Deseret Book, 1994.

———. *Key to the Science of Theology*. Salt Lake City: Deseret Book, 1966.

———. *A Voice of Warning*. Salt Lake City: The Church of Jesus Christ of Latter-day Saints, 1957.

"Preparing for Influence of Holy Ghost." *Church News*, 17 March 1990.

Roberts, B. H. *A Comprehensive History of The Church of Jesus Christ of Latter-day Saints*. 6 vols. Provo, Utah: Brigham Young University Press, 1965.

Robinson, Stephen E. *Believing Christ*. Salt Lake City: Deseret Book, 1992.

Romney, Marion G. Conference Report, April 1944.

———. Conference Report, April 1977.

———. "Revelation in Our Personal Affairs." *Relief Society Magazine*, October 1955.

Smith, Joseph. *History of The Church of Jesus Christ of Latter-day Saints*. Edited by B. H. Roberts. 2d ed. rev. 7 vols. Salt Lake City: The Church of Jesus Christ of Latter-day Saints, 1932–51.

———. *Lectures on Faith*. Salt Lake City: Deseret Book, 1985.

———. *Teachings of the Prophet Joseph Smith*. Selected by Joseph Fielding Smith. Salt Lake City: Deseret Book. 1976.

———.*Times and Seasons* 3 (15 June 1842).

Smith, Joseph F. *Gosepl Doctrine*. 5th ed. Salt Lake City: Deseret Book, 1939.

Smith, Joseph Fielding. *Answers to Gospel Questions*. Salt Lake City: Deseret Book, 1957.

———. *Church History and Modern Revelation*. Salt Lake City: The Church of Jesus Christ of Latter-day Saints, 1953.

———. *Doctrines of Salvation*. Compiled by Bruce R. McConkie. Salt Lake City: Bookcraft, 1954.

———. "Fundamental Gospel Truths Balance Education for Students at BYU." *Church News*, 4 November 1961.

———. *The Progress of Man*. Salt Lake City: Deseret Book, 1964.

Smith, Lucy Mack. *History of Joseph Smith by His Mother*. Edited by Preston Nibley. Salt Lake City: Bookcraft, 1958.

Snow, Lorenzo. Conference Report, 6 April 1900.

Stoker, Kevin. "Prophet Renews Friendships." *Church News*, 16 July 1988.

Stuy, Brian H., ed. *Collected Discourses*. 5 vols. Burbank, Calif., and Woodland Hills, Utah: B.H.S. Publishing, 1987–92.

Talmage, James E. *A Study of the Articles of Faith*. Salt Lake City: Deseret Book, 1983.

Tyler, Daniel. "Recollections of the Prophet Joseph Smith." Juvenile Instructor 27 (15 February 1892): 127–28.

Whitney, Helen Mar Kimball. *Woman's Exponent* 9 (1880): 18.

———. *Through Memory's Halls: The Life Story of Orson F. Whitney*. Independence, Mo.: Zion's Printing and Publishing Co., 1930.

Woodruff, Wilford. Conference Report, October 1897.

———. *The Discourses of Wilford Woodruff*. Comp. G. Homer. Salt Lake City: Bookcraft, 1969.

Young, Brigham. *Discourses of Brigham Young*. Selected by John A. Widtsoe. Salt Lake City: Deseret Book, 1941.

Young, Joseph. *History of the Organization of the Seventies*. Salt Lake City: Deseret News Steam Printing Est., 1878.

Index